I HAVE TO SURVIVE
MIRIAM'S STORY

MIRIAM GARVIL
Preface by Ruth Campbell

September, 2012

Copyright © 2012 Miriam Garvil

ISBN 10: 1479392790

ISBN 13: 9781479392797

I Want To Thank Ruth Campbell With All My Heart For Helping Me Write My Book.

MIRIAM GARVIL
SEPTEMBER, 2012

I HAVE TO SURVIVE
MIRIAM'S STORY

Preface

This book is a transcription of tapes Miriam Garvil recorded with me over many sessions in 1993–1994. Unfortunately, I didn't have time to do anything with it after it was first transcribed. I recently discovered the manuscript again and felt it was such an important story that it should be published so others could read it.

I have edited the transcript to give the narrative more coherence and remove some of the duplications, but basically this is the story Miriam told. She has recently worked with me to revise and update it. It is a powerful story of a young girl with a happy childhood whose life suddenly turned into a nightmare. The fact that she survived is a testimony to her strength, her will to survive, and her ability to think and move fast. It is also a miracle.

After reading this, I wanted others to read it and be moved as I was to hope that nothing like this will ever be allowed to happen again.

Ruth Campbell
September, 2012

Cover photo shows Miriam as a young girl dressed in her favorite outfit to look like a boy.

I HAVE TO SURVIVE

MIRIAM'S STORY

Table of Contents

Chapters . . . . Page

1. The Early Years 1

2. Times Change: The Beginning 23

3. Krakow-Plaszöw Camp 41

4. Birkenau and Auschwitz 63

5. Bergen Belsen 75

6. The End of the War 81

7. Julian, George, Paris, New York 89

8. After Julian's Death 103

Timeline 105

1 The Early Years

Lodz

[In the 1920s, the population of Lodz was 670,000 with a Jewish community of more than 230,000, the second largest in Poland. Jews dominated retail trade and operated more than half of the city's factories. The economic engine of Lodz was the textile factories.Yivo Institute, 2010]

I was born in Lodz, Poland, in 1921. All my life I lived in big cities. Ann Arbor was the first time I lived in a small town. I was afraid at first that I would not be able to get used to it, but when I came here I liked it. Our house in Lodz was a beautiful house that belonged to my uncle. There were maybe thirty-two tenants in a very big house. This was an

I

apartment that you buy, not rent. It was a big building with an entrance in the front and the back. The front was really very elegant, with marble steps and doors with crystal. Really, you don't see houses like that anymore.

When I was three, there was a fire in the factory about one block away; everything was red. I was terribly afraid. This stays in my mind. I was standing looking out the window in the room my sister and I shared. I had a sister who was three-and-a-half years older than me. This fire is in my memory. I was three years old then. I was afraid.

We lived on the third floor in a four-room apartment. A fun thing that I remember was that my parents let me shimmy a Charleston. They had a teacher I learned it from. Then when I was maybe six years old, my uncle went away to Bucharest, Romania. He left my mother to manage the building, which was very unusual at that time. None of my friends' mothers were working. Now women are working, but then, this was really something. We moved to my uncle's beautiful apartment.

My father owned a factory making wool material. We were very well off, you can imagine. Both my parents were working, and my father was very good at what he was doing. He always went away for vacations to the mountains, skiing. They always went somewhere for vacation. My mother went in the summer, and my father in the winter. He couldn't afford to go in the summer, because he had to prepare the stuff for his factory in the summer so the materials would be ready for the fall. He went to Warsaw very often to sell those materials. He had very good friends in Warsaw.

We went to a very good private school, which wasn't Jewish, but we had a Jewish teacher who came to teach us history. When I was a little bit older, I had to learn French and Latin. I hated Latin because it was a dead language.

I loved French. My dream was always to go to France when I got older. I eventually went to France but not the way I was dreaming about.

I remember that when I was young, my sister was very afraid of dogs. One day when she was very small, she went to a store where they sold milk and cheese and cream and vodka and things like that. And she was dressed in white cotton, completely in white, and the dog was sitting there and attacked her. She was very small, and she remembered it all her life. When she saw dogs, she always ran away. She was hurt just a little bit, not so bad, but it was the shock that stayed with her. I can never forget it. I didn't see it because she was a little girl and I was a baby—maybe I wasn't even born yet.

When my sister and I were small, we went to lodges in the summer. One day while we were there, my mother sent her to get bread. When she got there, she saw a sign in the front that said the store was closed on Sunday, and when she walked to the back, she saw a dog. When she came home without bread, she said, "In front it was Sunday, in back a dog." This became a big family joke. If someone couldn't do something, we would say, "Sign in front, dog in back."

I remember another funny thing. My mother sent my sister to buy cold cuts. She ran home, and she was ringing and ringing the bell without stopping. I opened the door. My sister was standing on the marble stairs, and a package came flying out. First came the package; afterward she came in. I said, "What happened?" And she said, "A dog was running after me because of the meat." She was afraid of dogs her whole life.

My mother was very busy; she had work, and she was with us constantly. My cousin who is now in Australia used to come to see her because he liked her very much. That cousin was very close to me. He came every week to our house. I recently got a letter from him. He wrote, "You have nobody, just us." It's true, his brother is also alive so I just have the two of them. This is the reason I am talking about going to Australia. That cousin who was so close to me has been very sick lately. I don't know if he's ready to have anyone visit now.

Their mother and my mother were cousins, so we are second cousins, but I don't think this counts; I think blood really doesn't count. There was something in how there was a connection between us when we were children. I remember him in our house very often. We always had a woman in my house helping my mother with cleaning, cooking, and shopping. My mother always had plenty of people for holidays and other times. My parents had many, many friends. The father of this cousin, he was very, very religious. He would never eat in our house. Kosher people can eat on glass, because glass is something they can even use on Passover. You can wash and use the same glass dishes. My mother would always give him a glass plate with an apple or something because he couldn't eat a meal in our house. This I remember very well. The younger cousin went to some special technical school. They weren't very well off, and my mother would try to help them. She'd give them materials from my father's store. The older son was the good one; he fed his parents; he always lived with them.

My cousin, the youngest one who lives in Australia, his parents had a kind of small summer house, near a lodge. We went and visited them very often, and nearby was a very big house like a chateau, and there was a young girl living there. My younger cousin was crazy in love with her. But he felt like he didn't fit with her. They were very rich people, always having parties and things, while he was in the background. This was the dream of his life. Always when we came there, he was talking about this girl. It so happened that during the war, my cousins went to Russia, running away from the Germans. From Russia they went to Australia, both my cousins, David and Kubat. David is the oldest, and he met a woman in Australia who had a child. Her husband, I think, was dead. He married her, and he was very happy. The son was like his own son. The son became a lung doctor, and he died of a lung sickness. Kubat couldn't find anybody to marry. After the war, somebody told him that I was in Paris. He wrote to Paris through the Joint (Jewish Joint Distribution Committee). From the Joint he had an answer about me that I went to the USA with my husband and my son. The woman who wrote to him was the girl of his dreams. She was married. I don't know what happened to her husband—if they divorced, if he died; I have no idea. But she wrote to him that she was living in Paris. She knew him, but she had ignored him before. Then he wrote to her saying, "How about coming to Australia, to Melbourne, and marrying me?" And she went. Can you believe it? It's like a movie story. Right now she is in big trouble. She had a stroke, and she can't move one hand and one leg. He's retired. He's the one who has to help her. We were thinking about going to Australia. Julian's [Miriam's husband] doctor said it's too long a trip for him. We were thinking maybe we'd meet in the middle, but she's not able to do that. He cannot leave her. That's why it's a little bit of a problem.

I had a very nice childhood.

Our life in Poland was very good. We had a good life. My mother was a very severe mother, and I think she loved my sister better than me because my sister was very studious. We were in classes from eight to three every day. Then we had homework until eleven at night. In Europe, study was study, not like here. You see, here you have it so easy. You have tests, they give you three answers, and you have to choose. I told my son George it was no way like that in Poland, nothing to choose. I had everything in my head, and I had to remember the right answer. I had to know without three choices. No choosing, I said. George didn't believe me.

I hated Latin grammar. When you like something, it becomes easy for you. This wasn't me. Drawing, color, French, I liked. Things that I didn't like, like Latin, couldn't come to me. You know what my mother did? She got my sister's teacher in gymnasium to teach me Latin so I'd be able to pass from class to class. In Europe, when you're no good in one subject, you stay the second year in the same class. I don't know what they do now, but when I was a girl they didn't let people pass if they failed a subject. I wasn't ashamed. I hated Latin. I told everybody. My teacher knew it. I said, "This isn't me." I couldn't put that in my mind. I didn't like it, and I didn't want it. French, I didn't make a fuss. It was lovely. I loved it.

I was happy in Paris. [Miriam went to Paris after the war when she married her husband.] You know why I was happy in Paris? This was a dream from my childhood. From the time I started learning French, I loved France. I was always dreaming that I was going to live in France. In Europe, school is different. You have four years of high school, and then you have two years of college. This two-year college is the *lycée*. You prepare yourself for what you choose. My sister finished two years before me. My mother said, "OK, you can both go to Paris," because my sister also wanted to go to France to learn languages. She was learning languages in Lodz, waiting for me, because my mother said, "No way you go alone. You have to go together." We were supposed to go together. We didn't want that. My sister after a time was doing different jobs with the French language and I think English too—different jobs in languages. My dream was to be in art, drawing, fashion, and draping, things like that. We were waiting to go to Paris but the war came and we never got there.

I like color. Even though I am old, I am very conscious when it comes to color, fashion. When something doesn't fit, I try to repair it because I don't like it. Even when I was very fat, I was like that. I was so fat I couldn't lose the weight. Life is really something. When you try to lose, you can't; when you don't want to lose, you lose. I was very thin when I was a girl. They gave me some special oil because I was so thin. I couldn't stand that.

My parents came from Russia. They ran away from Russia during the revolution. When they didn't want us to understand, they talked Russian. And we caught it. We knew it already, everything. I think I loved Russian and French, the two languages I really liked, because my parents were talking Russian very often. My mother took lessons for Polish in Poland because she needed it for her job. She was a teacher. And I liked music, but I didn't like to study it. We had a teacher, and she came twice a week, and we'd have to play the piano—me one hour, my sister one hour. I hated it. But when I grew older, I was very sorry that I hadn't put more effort into music, because I appreciated it more. I started to love it. You see, it was too much for children. They didn't realize that. I realize that now. We didn't have a half an hour to take it easy. We had a half day off on Thursday because we had to go skating. But I went skating early instead of doing homework first. It didn't go

7

to my mother's head that I cannot study when I don't have a little bit of relaxation. Today people understand that better. Then they didn't, and my older sister was very studious. She came home, we had a big meal, and she studied. I couldn't study. To me it was too much sitting for such a long time in class from eight to three.

I had many, many friends. You know what, I was really a dreamer. In Poland, when you had movie theaters on the street, they showed you many pictures from the movies. I was always telling my three girlfriends the plot of the picture. I remember when I was maybe thirteen, this was Madame Valenska, with Charles Boyer. He played Napoleon. And we had a big literary magazine. You could win things when you put the Madame Valenska sayings from the movie in order. I went to the movie with a flashlight. People were staring at me because I was using a flashlight to put the sentences in order. I was so happy. I won soap. I don't remember how much. This was almond soap. Now it's nothing, but in Poland this was special, a very beautiful smell, such nice pieces. I was so proud. I said to my mother, "You see, I am doing something good too," because my mother was criticizing me very much.

I remember one year I was saving my allowance. We had Easter vacation one whole week; I went every day to the movies. You know, there was a movie, *Lola*; it was "la la." I shouldn't have seen the movie. I knew my mother wouldn't be happy. By chance I met my mother's girlfriend there. But she didn't tell my mother. I was afraid she was going to say something, but she made like she didn't see me. I saw her later on, and she didn't say anything to my mother. I'll never forget, seven days in a row I went to the movies.

(*And your mother didn't know?*) She knew maybe three times, four times. You see, my father was spoiling me. He'd give me money; he even said sometimes, "Go ahead, take it from my jacket." My mother never did that. Everything was counted, for pencils, for books, for lunch. My father wanted a second child, a son, and I was born. He treated me like a boy. He took me to hockey games. I loved to watch hockey games. I don't like it here because they fight. In Poland, they didn't fight; it was just a smooth game. I loved it.

My mother taught me to skate. My parents, from Russia, they were skating hard. My mother was over thirty when, after sixteen years of not skating, she went to skate again. She didn't say anything to us about it; she was such a strong person. She found somebody who taught skating. She started to skate, to learn. She went right away with the teacher, maybe three times. And then she said one day, I remember like today, she said, "I am skating." My father didn't believe it. And we went, the whole family. We were all skating.

Very often we traveled to a big mountain. We had a very long sled, and my father was sitting in the end and then my mother, my sister, and me, and he was driving the sled like a horse, like a car. We had to walk up, up, up to go down for one minute, but we loved it. My father also taught me to swim. He was a terrific swimmer. In fact, he always told us he went to a gymnasium in Moscow, and the owner of the school, the director, his son was with my father together in class. He told me this story a hundred times. He said, "I was a better swimmer than him." But that boy would always win because he was the son of the director. He couldn't forget that in his life. I remember my father jumping off of high bridges into the water. He would swim when there was ice in the water. I never remember my father getting sick as long as he was alive. He was a very healthy man. We had a very nice childhood.

Except my mother always reminded me that school was so expensive. I should learn more, I should study more, you know. I neglected Latin, and she had to bring someone special to help me; it bothered me. I always felt that my mother loved me less than my sister.

My mother was such a strong woman.

We had a beautiful apartment because my uncle owned the house and had left it for us. In all the rooms, there was wallpaper. In the edge of each room, all around, was a golden frame. This was really beautifully done. We had carpets on the floor, and there were three rooms. One was mine and my sister's. There was a room where my mother had her desk where she worked with two big, high windows, and it was like a dining room. We didn't have a living room. In the dining room, there was a big table with twelve chairs. My parents' room was off the dining room.

I remember one day we broke the—ah, we had three balconies in our apartment, can you imagine? There were balconies from the small room where my mother was doing her work, from the kitchen, and from my parents' room. One day my parents went out. We were teenagers and we were running around, and we broke the door to the balcony in my parents' room. We covered it, but my mother saw. She was really very mad. I'll never forget that day when she said, "Just when I go away, you go crazy." My mother was such a strong woman you wouldn't believe it. One winter my father went skiing like every year, around Christmas until New Year, because this was the time when he could go;

I didn't see it before. It was the first time that maybe there was a little bit of an opening in the box where she kept special things. Usually this is a secret button—you cannot see that you can open it. I pushed it up and got out the clipping from the newspaper. I am reading "courageous," this and that. "WOMAN WHO HAS NO NERVE"—such a title you, wouldn't believe it. I sat and read the story, and that day came to my mind because I remembered there was some phone call from my father, then I found out everything. I said, "I know you're going to scream at me because I went through your box, but I wanted to know what it was." I called my sister, I showed her the paper, and my mother knew she had no way to get out of it.

She said OK and she told us the whole story. The police called her when they made a lineup. The guy from the police was holding my mother's hand. He said, "Don't talk when you see them; just squeeze my hand." She saw them, and she didn't squeeze. She was afraid. My mother said, "This was the first time in my life I was afraid something would happen to my kids. If they put them in prison, when they got out, maybe something would happen to us." She said, "I didn't touch the hand; I didn't squeeze it." And we found out the whole story that happened. My father was in Auschwitz (before the war, it was an elegant place with mountains for skiing), and he read what had happened in the newspaper and called my mother, asking if he should come back. She said, "No, everything is OK." But then she got scared and called him, and he came home early. This was fishy, I remembered later—the phone call with my mother talking to my father and him coming home early. I didn't pay attention then, and later I figured it out.

(*How much later did you find out this true story?*) Five years. You imagine? In the first moment, yes, she was angry, not because I found the newspaper, but she was angry because I was there. I dug through her box, jewelry and things. But afterward she said, "I think it's time you knew what really happened." And she told us the whole story. You should see what they wrote about my mother—that she has such nerves, that they never saw such a person. I'm telling you, she was a strong woman. You couldn't find a woman like my mother working as a manager in such a big house. This was some responsibility. Not just taking money. Like this washing—there wasn't a washing machine. She had everything in her head. There was a special place in the basement for coal because we had such a big chimney where you had to put coal to feed the rooms. Everyone had his own space. When coal was coming, my mother had to know that the super would be ready to take the coal to each apartment. This was a bigger responsibility than to be a manager today. I didn't realize that then; I realize that today. How she really was smart; not just that, she was always talking about those women who have nothing to do, just to make a new dress and sit in restaurants, but she couldn't stand that. She played poker, every second week, but funny thing: my father, he was always winning when they played. They had friends who came to play cards, and my mother said to him, "You shouldn't win in our house." She was feeling so bad, and my father said, "I can't help it if they don't believe I bluff." I always remember when they were talking about this.

We had a very good life.

(*She was a smart woman, your mother.*) Very… My mother really wanted to know everything. She was always finding out everything about what to do and how to do it. You know, she didn't know Polish, so she took a special teacher to give her lessons to be able to talk perfectly with people who were living in our house. She was born in Russia. The time when I was a teenager, you didn't see a woman like that. Really, you didn't. I was proud of her. Just one thing was between me and my mother. I felt she didn't approve of me. You see, she approved of my sister much more because when my sister came home, she ate dinner and then did her homework. I couldn't. We went to school at eight o'clock, we came home at three o'clock, and then we were supposed to do homework until eleven maybe. So much homework you wouldn't believe it. Sometimes I put my Latin book under my pillow thinking "Maybe this will go into my head," because Latin for me was murder. Anyway, my mother was really after us to study, and she thought first study, then pleasure. I felt I had to go skating a little bit to be able to work again. She didn't like that, but I did it anyway because I couldn't sit and do something when my brain didn't work. I needed some relaxation, music… Funny thing, I was reading a few days ago that people who study while hearing classical music do better than sitting in a quiet room.

I was a good student with things that I liked. With things that I didn't like, I wasn't. I was terrible at Latin. In Europe, I don't know now, but then you had to be satisfactory every-where, otherwise you didn't go to the next class. Here you can go to the next class; you do over just one subject. It wasn't like that there. You had to be good in everything you took; otherwise you spent a second time in the same class. My mother didn't want that, so she hired my sister's teacher to teach Latin at home. But things that I loved came so easy to me. I liked French; it was very easy. I liked drawing and painting, and those things were very easy.

We went to a very good school. We had winter vacation for two weeks with the teacher, going away just to look at nature and learn about nature. This was part of the class, and I loved this vacation in the winter. This was the most beautiful two weeks in the whole year for me. I was always waiting for those two weeks. We had a very good life. This was something. Really, my parents wanted to give us the best that they could. I don't think my parents talked much about their childhoods. My father talked about one thing: swimming. I mentioned before how he said he was the best in high school in Moscow. He loved sports. He went skiing; he went swimming; he loved it.

(Were you closer to your father than to your mother?) Much. He really did for me whatever I wanted. My mother said, "This is terrible. Whatever Mirka says, you do. Why do you spoil her like that?"

He said, "I don't know. I think you spoil Lonya so I like to spoil Mirka." He called me Mirka. He spoiled me not because she spoiled Lonya, my older sister. I think it was because I was the kind of girl that was like a boy, you know. I enjoyed hockey games when he took me, always. In fact, he had wanted his second child to be a son. Because he didn't have one, he treated me like a son. I have pictures of him. I had nothing after the war, just my cousin who was in Bucharest. She had some of our family pictures, many pictures that she gave me when I came to the family in Bucharest after the war. I have a picture of my father skiing, and when he wrote a letter to my family from his vacation place in Russia, I have that. My father was a very good-looking guy, six feet four tall, and he went on a diet then. He was eating graham rolls to lose weight. He wasn't fat. We had a girl who was cooking. She cooked a lot; the table was full. When he felt he was too fat, he went on the graham rolls and yogurt. This wasn't yogurt, this was buttermilk; he'd just take the cream off, and this was his diet. He loved to wear beautiful clothes. What went to the laundry had to come back with a very stiff collar. I remember if he didn't like it, he'd say, "This is not a good job." You know what, nobody believed he was our father. He looked very young. Sometimes when we went out together, they asked my father, "Is this your sister?" He liked that very much.

But my mother had more energy than my father, I think. She was working more. He liked very much to go out, have company. My mother stayed with us. This had to be done that way. It was a little bit too strict, I think. When I think back now, they wouldn't approve today of this kind of mother with her regime, you know. She didn't spank me. For me it was when my mother or my father said, "Mirka!" This was enough. I ran right away to our room, crying.

I had close friends, girlfriends, and I had boyfriends before the war. But you see, our apartment was so occupied. When Thursday afternoon was free, this wasn't free because we had swimming lessons, and one day a week we had kind of dancing lessons, not *dancing* dancing, rhythmic dancing. We were occupied. We didn't have time for things like … just one thing. I liked to talk for a long time on the phone, and my father, when he wanted the telephone, would always say, "I knew Mirka was on the phone—she likes to talk so much."

(*Did everyone have a phone at that time?*) No, no. You know, it's a funny thing. When I was living in New York, the lawyer from this company wanted the Germans to pay me something, compensation for the concentration camps. He asked me different things about my childhood. Funny thing, I had a car accident in '66, and I was talking with the lawyer, and she said to me, "If you were richer, they would give you more money. If you were Mrs. Kennedy, they would give you income compensation."

I said, "Why?" She said, "Because this is the way it is in America. When the same accident happens to Mrs. Kennedy and you, you cannot compare even what compensation she would have for the same kind of accident." Why am I telling you this? Because this guy, when I had an interview with him for this organization for the Germans and compensation, he asked me about my childhood, and I told him my father had a factory in Lodz. I said we had a phone. I even remembered the phone number—it was 1050. And he said, "This is not possible. Who had a phone in Lodz before the war?" And I said, "You'd be surprised how many people were rich." He didn't believe me. I have a friend who went to some special library. He found a book from Poland, before the war, with our telephone number. I made a copy and gave it to the lawyer. He said, "This is something." When I was bigger, they put in a red one, and the number was 10050. The number "1" was in red, and "0050" was written in black.

I said, "You see, you didn't believe me. I even remembered the number."

You had to be pretty well off to go to a private school in Poland. It was very expensive; it wasn't cheap, because you had real luxury. Thursday afternoons the school had swimming. Going on vacation in the winter for two weeks, this was from school. My parents also sent me to camp. When I was small, they took me with them on vacations. They usually took some kind of small summer house, and we went in the summer with my sister and my aunt, who didn't have kids. My aunt always went with us. Really my mother didn't like to go, you know, to sit in such a place for vacation. And she couldn't; she was working but my parents came to visit every weekend. This was fun, this place; really, we had fun there. And my mother went for two to three weeks to this other place to take kind of a cure, relaxation.

(*Was she sick?*) No, she had plenty with her job. You see, my father was a big flirt, and women liked him. My mother was very jealous; I had this feeling from childhood. He looked so young and so good, and she was very jealous of him. And sometimes I heard because our room and my parents' room, we had the same door. Sometimes I heard the way my mother was talking. "Why did he do that, why did he do that?" So she needed, really, to get away from everything. But I adored my father, I really did. Maybe because he spoiled me, I don't know. When I needed money, he didn't even ask me for what. He'd say, "Go and take it from my jacket, left pocket" or something. And my mother couldn't stand it. She'd say, "At least ask her what she needs it for. What can she need it for? Something for school or lunch or movie, we give her."

See, he didn't ask why I wanted the money. And he trusted me, so when he found out that I went one vacation— Passover vacation, I mean Easter—everyday to the movies, seven days, he would laugh, and my mother would want to kill me. That was the difference. You know, when they went to a movie, I didn't ask what kind of movie picture. I asked who was laughing. I knew that when my father was laughing, this meant it was a good, funny movie. When my father wasn't laughing, this was a drama, and my mother wanted to see that. This was some kind of thing that a child understands about her parents. I don't know, I wonder if George would have such a memory like I have from how it was between me and Julian. Because we never talked about it. To George it was completely different, because he was feeling very sorry that we went through such a bad time.

When George was older, he started to belong to the second generation of the Holocaust group. He was very interested. He was always talking about it. I was the kind of parent who talked a lot. Julian doesn't talk; Julian writes. But I talked a lot with George. This was important to him. One day his friend told him, "George, you need to go to a psychologist." He said, "I don't need it. I can tell everything I think to my mother." We were really very open. Friends, not just mother and son, you see. I was telling him things like not many mothers would tell a son.

Like I said to my father one day, "Why do you flirt?" My mother was suffering so much. Because it happened that we were alone; my mother was gone and my sister was gone. Sometime during the war, I said, "Why are you like that?" He said, "You know, men can love too."

I said, "Just men? Women cannot?"

He said, "I don't know, when you're older maybe you'll find out."

I said, "Men take love too many different ways." And I was talking about those same things with George. Like sometimes I didn't like the way he treated his girlfriends. "See," I said to George, "I am a woman. I feel the way she feels. Believe me, I know what I am telling you." I think he believed me. He never asked for advice. He'd say, "Let me learn from my own mistakes." But maybe it helped a little bit. I didn't see that. But we were very close. We were really open. We were talking to each other like friends, like old friends, and this I miss very much. I really miss him [George died in 1992].

(*Do you remember the names of any of your friends back there?*) Yes, Hanaka Schneider was my very, very good friend. You see, her parents and my parents were seeing each other very often. And we were very close, Hanaka and me. I think sometimes that she is in America. She went with her father to Russia. My father, when the Germans came to Poland, wanted to take me and go to Russia, toward the frontier. And he said to my mother and Lonya, "I'll send for you." My mother said, "No way. We all go together, or nobody goes." Maybe if he went, maybe he'd be alive. Because both my cousins who are now in Australia, they went to Russia. Then from Russia they went to Australia.

2 Times Change: The Beginning

This was the start of a very bad time.

Yes, things started to change; I'm going to tell you. In the summer of 1938, we went for a vacation. Do you know the educational system in Poland? I don't know now, but in Europe then there was a different system than in America. This was the year in which I finished those two years of *lycée*. I wanted to go to college for art, two more years, and then I wanted to go to France. My mother told my sister that she had to wait. She finished college before me, and she wanted to go to France to study languages, but I still had two years until 1940. I never did it because the Germans came in '38 to Poland. But she was ready to go. And we wanted to go to Paris.

I had never been to Paris. I just saw pictures, books. This was my dream, and my sister also wanted to study languages in Paris. (I went, but not the way I wanted.) And my mother said to her, "You study languages here as much as you can, and when you are ready, when Mirka is ready, you go together." We were waiting, and it never happened. Germans… And this is—I really don't know how to start to tell you.

In the summer of 1938, I went with my sister to a kind of camp for college students, and this was near Lvov in Poland. And we spent there—I don't remember, exactly—a few weeks, and I remember that when we went there, it had already started with Hitler in Germany. And some people were, you know, wise. They said next would be Poland. I had an uncle in Bucharest, a very rich guy. He had three factories, silk, linen and wool, I think. And everybody in the camp said, "We are not far from Hungary here. You could go to Hungary and go to Bucharest." And they asked me, "Why do you go back home? You'd better stay here; maybe something will happen." It was very bad already, hearing my parents say what Hitler was doing with the people, with the Jewish people. My mother said many people who were living in Germany and born in Poland were coming back to Poland.

I remember my mother came one day [before the summer camp] into our room and said, "Mirka and Lonya, you have to make packages. Whatever you don't wear, good things, we make packages and send them to Auschwitz." Auschwitz was the place with a concentration camp because this was on the frontier between Poland and Germany. Hitler just told them, oh, Auschwitz, this place. This was the beginning when they settled there. [Auschwitz opened as a camp in February, 1940. The first prisoners were German criminals, most of whom became kapos in the camp. The first mass transport came in June, 1940 with 728 Polish political prisoners from Tarnow. The first gassing of prisoners occurred in September, 1941.] I remember I was thinking whether to give or not to give, but you know how it is when it's not your skin. It's just, how do they say—"skin is more"—your feeling is more on your skin than on your coat. This was like my coat which I could take on or off. I was very sorry. I sent my stuff, but it wasn't the same thing as when I was feeling it on me, later.

And we went to this summer camp, and people said, "Don't go back," and they were right. Because we stayed near Lvov. This was—I've forgotten what the place was; it will come to my mind; it was a place where students went to camp. And we went back to Lodz. This was a mistake because not long after, the Germans came to Poland. Lodz is more on the frontier with Germany. In fact, Hitler had split Poland. The part where I was in camp, Hitler was there also, but he left it for the Polish government. Lodz he considered Germany. Why? Because it had many textile factories, and he needed it for the soldiers. Right away he made kind of a frontier for Germany. I remember they came one day to my father's factory. They took all this stuff that was there. They gave my father a paper, and they said, "This is for Schindler." And this was all; they just took it, and this was the start of a very bad time.

This was the start of the ghetto in Lodz. We didn't go to the ghetto; we ran away. But before we ran away, it was so bad. Everybody needed permission for work. Or else they took people and sent them wherever they wanted. We were already under some pressure because we could expect that any time, the Germans could come to our house and do what they wanted. I remember in Poland—I don't know if you ever saw—when we went to Switzerland, I saw in the museum, a porcelain museum in Geneva, those high chimneys; you know, on the bottom you put coal, and this makes a hiding room. And some of these things, you wouldn't believe it. This was part of the room decoration in Polish houses to make the room look nice. On the top were painted things like a crown. It was cold on the top, and my father put everything good like sugar on top so the Germans couldn't relieve themselves on them. The top was like a crown, and you couldn't see inside.

They never heated my parents' room, because my father couldn't sleep when it was hot. This was so cold you wouldn't believe it. The coal didn't come toward that part of the house. He never let them heat his room when he was sleeping, or he couldn't sleep. He liked cold. It's a good thing because this way, my father went and put all the food up on the chimney. The Germans, when they came, you wouldn't believe what they did, relieving themselves. We had such a storm that my father put other things to eat in a special room between the kitchen and dining room where on the wall you could open all the shelves.

(*Like a pantry.*) Yes, then my mother always had—I don't know if this is maybe from Russia she had it, I don't know—like a big pot. You put gelatin in it and you make preserves. It has to be hot to have water boil in it. Here it is different. Here you do this automatically. My mother had plenty of those pots, and my father had tried to put all these big things on top in the chimney. He put things there in the top in case some people came. A few times Germans came. They were looking for something.

(*Did you understand then how bad this was?*) Sure, I was a teenager then. Sure, we knew that's why my father wanted to run away, and my mother said, "No, our whole family or nobody." And I started to work for—I think this was a Jewish organization, for art. They were doing drawing, sewing, things like that. We had a friend who was president of the organization, and she took me and gave me the kind of job that I would like, with colors, with materials. This way I had permission to go to work, and if someone stopped me, German soldiers or something, I'd say I was going to work. This was the beginning.

(*How did they know you were Jewish?*) I don't know; they were just stopping people on the street. We didn't even live in a Jewish neighborhood. Even for traveling we had checkpoints, you know, like they have on trains. And they always asked for identification. When you had a work card, it was OK. This was the beginning. Then came the announcement that all the Jews were supposed to wear a yellow star, a Jewish star. You had to cut it out yourself in yellow material. You had to make it yourself. In the beginning I didn't do it, and my mother was very nervous. When I went out, she said, "Why don't you do it?"

I said, "Because they are going to beat me." I didn't look Jewish, I said; I didn't have a big nose, you know, and I said, "Well you wanted me to go out, to go to work; I'm not going to put the star on." And my sister started to go out with the star. It wasn't OK. The Germans were always kidding her, and you know, telling stories. She was very nervous, and she stopped going out at all. I said to my mother, "See, if this is how it is, I don't want to do with the star."

We had to run away from Lodz.

We started to hear stories, beatings on the street, and my father said it was time to go away. They started to make a ghetto, and he said, "We are not going to the ghetto." My father's vision was very clear. He said we would starve in the ghetto. There was nothing to eat, no work. He said,

"We have to go." And where did we go? I told you that part of Poland was under the Polish government and part was the German government. And you couldn't go from one part to another without permission. Then my father said that we had to go now, you know, that we had to prepare. The whole family wanted to go. I had an uncle in Poland who was very, very rich. He said he could not go; he had to make a kind of safe place that he could put his money in. He put it in old furniture on the bottom, and nobody knew it. I remember how our girl who was working for us was sewing my father's fur coat and hiding money and jewelry inside. It was stupid because they took the fur coat right away.

We ran away from Lodz because it was very bad there. Right away the Germans came to Lodz because there were many materials there. They really needed cities in Poland with the possibility to grow, like in Germany. Warsaw was still Poland under the German government, but Lodz was made like a city that belonged to Germany. It was tougher; they made the ghetto faster, everything. And my parents didn't want to go to the ghetto. In fact when we heard about the Germans coming to Poland, my father told my mother, "Let's run to Russia." Then he said, "You know what, I'm going to America. You stay with Lonya (my sister) at home; I'll send for you."

And my mother said no way. "We all go together, or we just stay here." Funny thing, the same thing happened much later in France. Julian received a visa to America from his uncle. Julian said to me, "You know what, I'll go for one year to America. I'll see how it is, and then I'll send for you and George." I said, "Oh, no, we'll go together, or you'll stay." And we went together. At first it was tough; I was crying that I left Paris. Julian knew a little bit of English; I didn't. And it was really tough. We didn't know one thing. His uncle, who was an old guy already, was reading the newspaper. Julian, you know, was in aviation. "This is a big thing in America," his uncle said. "With your profession, having a degree from the Sorbonne [the historic and prestigious University of Paris], I'm sure you'll be able to find a good job."

But he didn't know that you had to be an American citizen to work for the government for this kind of job. And we came, and Julian couldn't work in what he was doing. It was tough for us because in the beginning he was working in things that really weren't for him. He was very unhappy. I took a part-time job. It wasn't good in the beginning. We sent George to kindergarten in New York, and then I took him back because he wasn't happy there. We couldn't go back. That was the worst thing. We had sold our apartment in Paris. To keep an apartment in Paris is very tough. A second thing: Julian had a government job in Paris. He had to sign that he had no permit to come back to this job, because it was secret; and he signed the paper.

Anyway, my mother did one very smart thing. She put her diamonds inside the buttons of her pajamas. You know, the whole preparation was so long that—I don't know if you recall, if you've ever learned about this history of what was happening in Poland, but in one moment the Russians came to Poland, and they took this part that wasn't German. So part was German and part was Russian. This was tough to go to the frontier between the German and the Russian parts. We were planning for part of the family to go to this small city, Dzialoszyce [it was then in the Russian part and had a large Jewish community], first and part to go soon after. And my mother, the way she was, said, "Am I going?"

And my sister, who was the good sister ... I want to tell you something on me. I felt my mother loved her more than me. She left with my father to go to Dzialoszyce; afterward I will tell you why. I said, "No way I am leaving my mother alone," even though my sister was the favorite one. And my father went with my sister. He was wearing the coat with fur on the inside and on the collar.

Anyway, I was staying with my mother maybe two or three weeks more, then we went. It so happened that before the war, my mother's family was all in Russia. Before the war, the police gave permission to people to leave, to visit family in Russia, and she brought so many things with her, you wouldn't believe it, dolls and things—to Lodz, and when she came to the Polish frontier, they took everything and said "No way do we let you go in like that. You can't bring gifts." But she was a very smart woman, and she brought so much, very much money. And she asked, if she was not able to take her things, could she go back later, and they said yes. I remember that because she had to bring everything back. I wanted to keep things, and my mother said no. Why I remember that is because she had a Russian passport. And because of that, when we went during the war from Lodz to Dzialoszyce, she had a Russian passport. You wouldn't believe the Russian woman who was looking at us, me and my mother. They didn't look at anything on my mother; they even left her fur coat because she had a Russian passport. But me they made naked. My mother said, "But this is my daughter."

They said, "Never mind, she was born in Poland. You are Russian." You believe it? I remember it like today. When they left my mother's fur coat, I was shocked; and me, they took everything from me. We went on from there to Dzialoszyce.

(*What did you wear?*) I don't recall exactly, but they just took it off and said I had to go for inspection.

And then we went to this place outside of Dzialoszyce which belonged to another part of our family. You see, this was kind of a family of ours. Rather, this was Julian's family, but we were family because Julian's sister and my cousin, my uncle's son who was living in Poland, were married in Prague. Julian's sister was studying in Prague. My cousin came back with her, and they were arrested because he was working for Trotsky, and they said he was a Communist. They sent him to Russia with his daughter and wife. And later she came back to Poland, and this was tragic.

Her husband's mother was my father's sister. My mother was really very nice to her. Her name was Klara, and her daughter's name was Zosia. She came with a small baby. They were living in Siberia; you know, he had a very good job in engineering, building bridges. But then somebody said he was working for Trotsky, and they killed him (they wanted to kill Trotsky). I remember she was in our house, and she was calling Russia to be able to talk with her husband, and they let her. And then later she found out they had killed him. They sent her back to Poland, and they killed her husband, my cousin. It's a good thing my aunt didn't survive, because I have another cousin, her other son, who went to Israel, and he died of tuberculosis. I say good thing she didn't survive to see all that. They sent my aunt to Auschwitz. Because now I see that for a mother to survive the death of her son, there is nothing worse in this world. After the war, I was saying, "Good, she didn't survive," because this was no good.

A year in Dzialoszyce City

OK, then we were in this small town for some time. I cannot recall exactly, maybe one year. And this was better because the Germans weren't interested in us. You know, it was a small place, and like Lodz, it was very commercial. Julian's family, the family of the sister who we went to, they had tremendous land and all outside the city—whatever you wanted, cows and horses—and they were living very, very well. Julian's two cousins were the owners. We had an apartment in a house near their place, but we always went there and spent all our time there. When the Germans came, they found out about all the things that they had there, and we had to go away. We went from that place to the nearby city, and we were living in just one room—can you believe that? Four people.

I met another guy in Dzialoszyce, that small city, and he's now a big judge in Israel, a really important person. This guy you have to admire. He was from a very poor family, very uneducated. He really made himself what he is now by working hard, by being willing to be somebody. I felt the force of him then, that he'd be somebody if he survived. Because you saw it, the way he pushed himself always, the way he was talking. Sometimes you felt about people who you saw, the way they pushed themselves, that they'd be somebody. He was a type like that. This is his name: Justice Moshe Bejski. When we went to Dzialoszyce, to the city, we lived near his family. He came very often to visit his family. I felt then that the guy, really—he was from a very poor family; his father was a tailor I think. I felt he'd be somebody; there was so much in him. And when I found out he is now in Israel, a big shot, I said, "Good for him."

(*This was a Russian city?*) No, no, this was still Poland. You see, Germans came, and it started to be German. You know, we were living fairly free before anybody came—a quiet, small city. The Germans came to the Jews and said, "You do whatever we tell you." They started moving people into small rooms, just in a few streets, you know; slow, slow, slow. And then there was deportation. We heard that they were killing people, putting them in ovens. And one day my father said he heard that, and my mother wanted to kill him. She said, "Why are you telling such a story?" He said, "I wish this was a story."

The train

And they put us in the train, a train for animals, in September during the Jewish holidays. They chose the strong, good-looking men for labor. They took my father there. I went with my sister and my mother, waiting for this train. This was fall 1939. It was hot, nothing to eat, nothing to drink. We were waiting for this train; I'll never forget that. This was an animal train, nothing, just a big door that you close with, you know, a small opening up on the side. We were all jammed in; they pushed us onto this train. Aha, they said you could take small packages; not many things, just a little. They wanted us to believe that we were going someplace else to live. They didn't tell us we were going to die. And we were there maybe three days. I remember the train would stop sometimes, maybe for fuel. I remember people were giving us water or something to eat through those small holes. It was so hot; there were maybe 120 people in one car. In the end we didn't have water to drink. People were drinking each other's urine. You wouldn't believe it. When I am talking now, I think, "This wasn't me; this was something that I was seeing, that I was observing; it wasn't me."

I was eighteen. And you know, I was thinking, "I don't want to live anymore." It was such a … It was terrible. My mother said, "Never mind, we'll come to someplace. It'll be OK." She was always optimistic … to me to look at all those people … I couldn't drink urine like they were doing; I couldn't even though I was so dry. My tongue was like wood. You heard my tongue move in my mouth. I came to my mother; I came to my sister; I said, "I'll jump."

My mother said, "Are you crazy?"

I said no; I couldn't stand it. I wanted to kill myself. And my mother said, "Don't do that. Don't do that," and I jumped from the train, from the small hole. I went to the man near the small window. It was up high in the train. I asked the man if I could stand on his shoulders, and I climbed up and jumped from his shoulders through the small opening. Half of my dress stayed in the train.

I tell you I jumped to kill myself, but I didn't die. I heard two shots. Germans were shooting after me. There was one German in the second van. There were 10,000 people in this train. They say many people jumped and nobody lived. My head went to the side, and I lost consciousness. I woke up in a dark room, and I heard a voice. I was found in a place fifteen minutes from Rava-Ruska, where there was a crematorium where they took people and killed them. But we didn't know. I jumped fifteen minutes from that. We didn't know we were going there. When we saw our father taken to the work camp, we were thinking they would take us to a work camp also.

I heard people talking. I was thinking they were Germans. I started to scream, "I am not Jewish!"

A guy came to me; it was so dark I couldn't see him. He said, "We know you are Jewish; we are Jewish too. We are Jewish, Polish side—jail men, bankers, police, and we are supposed to help Germans put the people in the train to send them to the crematorium. But we do what we can to postpone or hide these people." He said, "Don't worry, we will hide you because two Polish peasants saw you jumping. They came to us and said, 'We'll give this woman or this man to you, whoever was jumping, because we know you'll take this person to the crematorium.'" The Jewish men paid the Poles, I don't know, I can't tell you what, but they paid them to keep their mouths shut. They told me I was unconscious for three days. When I woke up, the guy was talking. You wouldn't believe it; I recognized something. I knew the voice. This was one of the students who was in the student camp with me and my sister. And many of those students were Jewish-Polish.

First of all he made me papers so that I could stay there, and then he put me in a house outside Rava-Ruska with some Jewish family who were leaving Rava-Ruska. You see, when the train came there and it wasn't full, they would catch people from there to make the train full to the crematory. Whatever he knew, because he was a policeman, he always told Jewish people in advance. Then he took me to the place where he worked. It was not a bad thing; he left me there. He said, "Don't talk and don't scream. I'll come back with the others." He was saving as many Jews as he could and hiding them. I heard people screaming and people crying. I tell you, I was sitting there thinking that any moment the Germans would come here. This happened a few times.

I wrote a letter to this guy who had the bookstore in Dzialoszyce telling him that I was alive, that I jumped from the train. [This man was a powerful person in the Jewish community in Dzialoszyce and the Germans left him alone. He was a friend of Miriam's family.] I couldn't write much because I was afraid. I told him I would tell him what happened if we ever saw each other. He paid some peasants to bring me back to Dzialoszyce. The man in Rava-Ruska was thinking, "She's Jewish; she can't go back to Dzialoszyce," and he knew my father was in a work camp and I couldn't see my father—we didn't know what happened to him.

But I did go back. I remember when the peasants came to get me. They told me to take a potato and make my hands and face dark because they were white, and then I'd look like a peasant. And they gave me such a haircut— don't ask. I was sitting there; I was so afraid because, you know, someone could come and say, "You are no peasant." Anyway, I went with these two peasants back to Dzialoszyce city. I had to live in this apartment with this guy from the bookstore (he was a big shot) because they were so squeezed there that the old room where my family lived was already taken. He said once to me, "You know, they are saying, the Gemeinschaft [the Jewish association that was working to save and hide fellow Jews], that we really can maybe bring your father back from this labor camp."

I made a mistake when I said OK. This was the biggest mistake in my life. Because men who were in the camp with my father, I met them after; these men survived. A few of those men are here in New York. They were working with my father. I told the guy from the bookstore, "OK, bring him back." This was the biggest mistake. I didn't realize that after this transportation to Dzialoszyce, there would be another transportation to Auschwitz. The day he left, my father wrote a few letters; the rest of his papers he threw from the train window. He sent a card addressed to me to this Polish woman who ran a butcher shop in Dzialoszyce; she was a friend of my family. The card said, "Maybe we don't see each other again." And they took him to Auschwitz. I never saw my father, because they took him to labor—but this wasn't labor; this was Auschwitz to be burned. Young people they took to work, sent to Dusseldorf to work. But in Dzialoszyce they took just those people who were looking tall and healthy, men mostly, to work. And he didn't look like he could work. They told him it was the train to Auschwitz. I don't know how long he was in Auschwitz. I received the card a short time after he left because if he had been in the concentration camp, I couldn't have gotten such a letter. In my imagination he just put it out the window and some-body…He wrote everything up, addressed it to the butcher lady, and they put it in an envelope so I got it.

Now, aha—the two Polish guys from Rava-Ruska who came to see me, they started talking again about the concentration camps, about the Germans sending people there. If we didn't want it, they said we should go someplace to, you know, to some Polish house or someplace like that which the Germans didn't know about. The guy from the bookstore, he knew the two people who took me from Rava-Ruska. They put me some-place, in a Polish family's house, outside Dzialoszyce, on the roof. They thought I'd stay there because everybody was hop-ing the war would finish. One thing I forgot to tell you: before transportation my mother took…She knew about transporta-tion. I think she believed in this killing, but she didn't want us to think it was true; that's why she was screaming at my father. When my mother went to transport, she left jewelry and things with a Polish woman who had a butcher shop. She said, "Whatever happens, when we come back, then you will give it back to us." She said, "I heard about them sending peo-ple away. If we disappear, this is yours."

Why am I telling you that? This came back in my mind because when I was in this place, on the roof, the man's wife always said, "Why is she sitting here and we get nothing for her?" I said, "Wait, I'll bring you something." I said to him, "One day, you know what, I am going to Dzialoszyce. I'll take some of my mother's watches and jewelry, and I'll give them to you. Your wife should not be talking like that." He said, "Don't go, it's dangerous."

I said, "No, this woman would never give it to you. I have to go." I put on my kerchief to cover my head, and I went there to see this woman. She said, "Mirka, what are you doing?" (They called me Mirka.) "You know they'll recognize you." You know, this was really courageous, when I think now, to go back there when there were no Jews anymore—just a few people from the Jewish organization.

I said, "I don't care. I had to go out from the Polish man's house. He doesn't want to keep me. You have to give me some jewelry from my mother. I'll give it to him, and he'll give me lodging." I said, "What do I care if someone catches me here or catches me there? I'll have to leave his house if I don't give him something." And she gave me—I don't remember what. I came back, and he took me back.

Then, while I was in the house of the Polish person, in the attic, one day he told me I had to go out from his house. What happened: one of the peasants who brought me to Dzialoszyce from Rava-Ruska, he saw me once, because the guy who was hiding me sometimes said, "Go down for a little bit; nobody's around. Just to have fresh air, you know." And this guy saw me, and came to him and said, "I am going to the Germans to tell them you have a Jewish woman in your house."

And he came to me and said, "I am sorry, you have to go with me to Krakow." I said, "What is in Krakow?"

He said, "They have a ghetto, special for Jewish people. You can live there." I didn't have a choice. Then I went with him for a little drive. And in the end, he left me there. I went to the Jewish ghetto.

Later I found out he had a Jewish family there, very rich, and he built them something in his basement, and they survived the war in his house. You see, God punished him. One week after the war, he died with this money that the Jewish people left him. Because his wife wrote to me, "My husband died." I wrote a letter to this butcher woman, and she wrote me too that he had died.

Why do I come back to it? Because when I was in Krakow-Plaszöw, I met this woman from Dzialoszyce. I told you about how the Germans wanted money, gold, and everything that people had. This Jewish woman in Krakow-Plaszöw said she had to give everything away. We were sleeping two people on each, they're called, *prycza*. A *prycza* [a three-tier wooden bunk bed] is something that is a long piece of wood, and you put pieces of wood in between, and you sleep on it. The woman who I was sleeping with was from the same small place where we had lived, Dzialoszyce. She lived there for some time with her parents. And she was also very fast thinking. There was a young German soldier who came to take her to transport. And she had a diamond. She said, "Look, take this diamond, and I'll run; don't look." And she ran away. She didn't go to transport.

But in the end, everybody ended up in the concentration camp. Whatever you had done before, you tried to run away, you tried to go, but you ended up in the camp. Money didn't help, because my parents had money. If they had thought in advance to arrange to pay someone we would maybe have survived. But not just that, during the war I told you I went with my sister to the camp where there were young students. They warned us that Hitler had started to approach Poland. This was near the frontier of Hungary and Poland, and then after that there was Romania. We were saying that we had a very rich uncle in Bucharest. They said, "Why do you go back to Lodz?" Because Lodz was really where the Germans would come right away, the way it happened. "You should go to your uncle, to Bucharest." And this was a mistake, you know, that we didn't go. We were just young women.

3 Krakow-Plaszöw Camp

I didn't stay in the ghetto long, because people who went from Krakow to the ghetto, they had apartments, they had their things, and they could survive. I had nothing. I knew I couldn't survive. When I arrived in the Krakow ghetto, there was ghetto "A" and ghetto "B." "A" was for people who had been living in Krakow, and "B" was for people from outside, people like me who didn't have anything. And "B" was terrible. There were many people in one room. I don't know how many people were sleeping on the floor. It was really very bad. We didn't have anything to eat—nothing; it was terrible. OK, after, when I went to the camps, I saw this wasn't so bad, but then it was terrible. You know, I had lost everybody; I was alone for the first time in my life, and I really didn't know what to do. They told me they had started to build a concentration camp, Krakow-Plaszöw, near

Krakow. I didn't know what for; I didn't know anything. I saw this as one way I could survive. I was thinking that I had, you know, a little bit of money.

I went voluntarily because we heard when they opened the Krakow-Plaszöw camp that the people who were willing to go there could have a better life. And we were thinking—we were foolish you know; we didn't know what to think then. Then those of us who were sleeping on the floor and had nothing, we said, "What can we risk?" We didn't realize we could risk a lot by pushing ourselves to go to Plaszöw. The conditions there were that we all had just one soup a day, but everybody had a few dollars, and we could manage somehow. I had some from my mother's jewelry. I had a few dollars, not much.

But I forgot to tell you something. When I jumped from the train, half of my dress stayed in the train. This means that after I jumped, I had just half a dress up top, no bottom. Then this guy who was taking care of me, he had to bring me a dress. Why I am talking about this is because it was a red dress. It was shocking for me to wear this dress in such a time. I said, "Red dress?" He said, "I have nothing else. You want to wear something that you will be working in. This is something that fits you." And I put on this red dress. I went with the red dress to the concentration camp. That's why I remember the red dress.

Work in the camp

Can you imagine, when we were in Krakow-Plaszöw, in this concentration camp, there was a Jewish cemetery. You know the first thing they gave us to do? To destroy the Jewish cemetery. This was Krakow-Plaszöw camp. They sent people there who wanted to go voluntarily, for work, they said. I was thinking maybe we were going for work. Our work was to destroy the Jewish cemetery. The big German in charge of the camp, Amon Goeth, came. He said, "Now we are going to destroy this cemetery. I will make the Jews cut these stones." And from these stones, he made a pavement which we were walking on in the concentration camp. We were sitting there and we were cutting, you know, such heavy things, the stones. Can you believe it? And we had there a couple of men and the big German. He was always very fat, very big. He always came on a horse to look from far away at what we were doing. In the beginning they were giving us soup twice a day and stuff like that. There were men who were working in the cemetery, but they were also going out to work in Krakow, in the city. When they came back, they brought in bread and things like that and gave other people the extra things that they were bringing.

Goeth was, I tell you, always on the horse. He had horses, and he needed the horses for his personal use, not just for the army. They were talking that he was a very mean person. I didn't know he had made big parties in his house with important Germans until I read about it in this book [*Schindler's List* by Thomas Keneally]. There was something wrong with this guy, some kind of sadism. I don't know how to tell you. He had a servant, Jewish, and he didn't want anybody to know she was Jewish. You know, when other people came from the outside, some knew it, people from Krakow, but when people came from far away, they didn't. We all had to wear the yellow star, and she didn't. They talk in the book about her, terrible things. He carried her once by her hair; he was really a sadist. You see, it is very familiar to me because I was there.

And then we were sent to different places to work. My first job, as I said, was cutting stones in the cemetery, then they could make the road we could walk on. Then the second thing was making straw mats that you use in the entrance of a house. We were working on a contingent when you have to do so many a day. Then they sent me to *Strickerei* [a knitwear factory] where we were making new socks or repairing old German wool things—socks or things like that. Not just army clothes, they were bringing tremendous bags with sweaters, socks, underwear, you know, tricot. It was bloody, with holes, and we had to repair them, cut out the bloody parts, and put in the patches. Or all the socks that were torn on the bottom, you had to make a new bottom. Then there were a few guys who were doing those new parts on the machines; and we were sewing one good part to one old part on the machines; this was our job. And it also was a contingent. This contingent was terrible. 150 pieces a day, attach one stocking to another. I just attached one pair to another. I attached it with one stitch; I didn't go all around.

"Who has done that?" the guard said. He said he'd kill us, but he didn't. You have to think there to be alive.

For sleeping, there was just a square piece, a long piece of wood. You put pieces of wood in between; you lay on it. This was a bed, [a *prycza* in Polish]. And we were sleeping two in each. The woman who was sleeping with me, she was lucky. Her husband worked with leather. People who knew how to work with leather had much better support than anybody else from the Germans. They wanted—they needed these people. They wanted them to work for them. And that's why they gave them things that they didn't give to other people. And not just Germans outside, Germans inside—the big shot, Goeth. You'll see him in *Schindler's List* for sure.

They sent us to different places to work to repair the stuff for soldiers like woolen things, sweaters, socks, and things like that. Afterward it was the *Wascherei* [laundry] for washing all the bloody stuff from the German soldiers and there was also the *Schreinerei* [sewing workshop] where they were sewing stuff that was supposed to be repaired. But the best place to work was in the kitchen.

(*What were the relationships like between other people, among the prisoners?*) We tried to help each other. When we came back from work, working all night, they needed blood. Do you believe it? They took Jewish blood to give to the army. You believe it? The Jews who they could not stand, they made them die. They took blood from us, from these young people. They were chasing us to take the blood. They said, "This is nothing. We just take blood. You drink water; you'll have your blood back." They knew very well we were not eating properly, and this wasn't like just nothing.

And we were running away from them. They saw us running one way. There was a sign on one block saying this was where the Germans were taking blood, but then they'd go to another block, but we went the other way. And in the end, they never caught me; they didn't touch me. You see what I mean? This was the way we were. You see, somebody who didn't have an open eye in the concentration camp isn't alive today. I have one girlfriend who another girlfriend helped because the first girlfriend's brother was her fiancée. If she didn't have her help, she wouldn't have survived, because she wasn't so fast. She couldn't see all over what you're supposed to do in the moment to be able to survive. To survive, you had to look all around you and be very observant. In the beginning, I didn't know if I wanted to survive the war. But this is just human instinct; you do that with instinct—you run.

(*Did you believe you'd survive?*) Yes. Yes, funny, I did. And I had that from my father, you know. He used to say, "I am going to survive." When I found out he died, I said, "I have to do this for him." I did everything possible to survive, really. But you know, this running around after working all night, this was murder. The men were doing those parts, I told you—the new parts of the socks, the new bottoms, and we were attaching the old parts. If they found out we weren't working with the machines, then they'd send us to another job. You wouldn't believe it. This used to be a house with two, three floors, wooden floors. Now this was an empty house without floors. It was just full with bags of tricots, things from the army in bags. We had to sort them out—what is good for cleaning, what is good for sewing, what is good for repairing, and we were sitting in the big house on the top of these bags and taking one bag out after another. It was winter, very, very cold. In between doing what they wanted, we were sewing panties, underwear, and putting them on us.

Runaway

Then I met a woman, Olga. I had met her really in the small city, Dzialoszyce, and when we went to the Krakow ghetto, she was with me there. We went together to Krakow-Plaszöw, and she was lucky. She knew terrific German, and they took her right away to the office, and she was working for the Germans. I don't know, there was a different story with her. I heard very bad things. I remember in New York, her husband came to our house, because we had met in New York. Once he came alone, and he told me how Olga had survived in a better way. I didn't have the courage to tell him what I had heard about her. I said she was lucky, that she knew good German, you see, because he was from Germany. I said, "You know, she knew terrific German. I took French, she took German in school. They took her because she was good."

There was something in her thinking where she was not cautious—you know what I mean? But she didn't talk with him about it. They had two daughters, but I don't think their life was happy. Anyway, why am I talking about that? One day she ran away from the camp. They didn't catch her. Her sister was living in the ghetto. She was disabled; something was wrong with her leg and she couldn't walk normally, so they didn't take her to the camp. A German came to the ghetto and brought her sister to camp, and they were beating her to force her to tell where Olga was. She really didn't know. Olga ran away; she was lucky she survived. She never talked about where she went. But they killed her disabled sister.

You know what the guy did, the big shot German, Goeth? He was always on the big horse, this big guy. Because what happened, they took four people from the camp and hung them to show what happened to people who ran away. And they made us stand and look at the bodies, hanging. I'll never forget that because it was the first time. After that, a hundred different worse things happened, but this was the first time when they told us to come look at those four bodies hanging. When I hear sometimes, on radio, some hanging thing, right away this picture comes to me. This was such... You know, you start to think about the guillotine. Right away comes this thing for me, the whole picture with these hanging people and the hard voice in German saying, "This is what happens to you when you run away from the camp." This is something that you live with. You cannot take this picture away from your eyes.

That's why I remember her, because she survived. I saw her in New York. She didn't tell me where she went. I don't know. In the beginning she was in the camp; after, I don't know if she was in another concentration camp. I really don't know. I remember this hanging. This is such a picture that will never go away.

(*Did she know about what happened?*) I think so because they took her sister. There was something wrong with her leg. This was the reason she didn't go to the camp. Because she was afraid that when she came to camp, they would see the way she walked and they'd kill her right away. Then she was sitting in the ghetto thinking, "Whatever happens, happens." But they brought her and beat her because of her sister, and Olga must have heard what happened. She had remorse, I'm sure. She couldn't know that, you know. And I don't know. In such circumstances you can't blame anybody. When I was in camp, I was thinking about those Jewish compromisers who were working for the Germans. This is another story about a whole group of Jewish people who were working for Germans to help us. You see what I mean? Germans didn't know what they were doing for us while they were working for them. There were many other people who were working just to save themselves. Anyway, these people who were working just to save themselves they ended up the way we all ended up. But in those circumstances—after I am now sitting here and thinking, after the war—maybe when a person has the opportunity to think "I'll survive this way," they don't care about others. They think, "When I can survive this way, then I am going to do what the Germans tell me to do because this is one way I can survive."

Everybody was thinking, "I survived. I survived the way I could." You know, the one guy from Krakow with his wife, you wouldn't believe it. He was like the king in

Krakow-Plaszöw, a Jewish guy. Because the big-shot German, Goeth, gave him support. He knew everything bad that the German wanted to do to us because he knew his mentality; he thought he was going to survive. And he was so nice to the German, doing everything that he told him to do, bad things to us. Then Goeth really gave him freedom to do a lot. This man was taking money from people. He really was living like a king. He knew how bad Goeth was, but he kept working with him, telling him things that he needed to know. A sad story that it worked this way.

(*Did he survive?*) I don't think so. I don't think so.

The movie *Schindler's List*, this whole story is about Krakow-Plaszöw. You see, Schindler, he took people from Plaszöw to his factory which was in Krakow. He helped them. The whole thing is about Krakow and the concentration camp in Krakow. For sure, for sure I want to see the movie. I am curious how they describe it. I have the whole interview with the guy who's doing the movie. I knew about it. I taped the interview. But sure I am going to see the movie.

Survival

What we were doing in between was sewing panties and gloves for ourselves because we didn't have any; we had nothing there. Then during the work, they left us there the whole day. And we had to do again and again the same thing—so many bags to be ready this day for washing or repairing, whatever. And when we were finished, we never said we were finished. We were doing things for us. But we were not just doing things for us. You asked about how I had money; we were doing things because we were working with the guys who were going out for work in Krakow, to the city. And German soldiers went with them to manage them—they were always watched. They went out for work from the concentration camp. They were finishing the ghettos and things; there was a lot of work in the city. The guys went out in the morning and came back in the evening.

They went with the Germans because this was work for Germans. But those Germans those that went with them were friendly with them. They knew that they brought back bread and things from work to the camp. And then what I was doing, not just me but all of us—when we were sitting there, we were sewing. We knew that nobody in Krakow, even Polish people, had woolen panties, woolen gloves; that's what we were sewing. Then we put the clothes on and went out to the barracks. When they came back from work, we gave them the things to sell the next day outside, and they brought us bread and money and things like that. This is the one way we survived. OK, not everybody. I told you: people who came from Krakow, they had money and jewelry.

I didn't have much. So we were doing these things. And this was terrific, because you sat there the whole day, you were sewing, you were doing something for yourself. You knew when you could have a piece of bread. And in the evening, you came to the barracks, and this was the end of the day. But this wasn't long. I don't know why, but they were changing things all the time. Suddenly we heard an alarm, everybody came out, and they took us places to show us how they killed other people. They made us watch. These people had to make their own holes, then after they were shot, they went down into the holes they had dug. And they made us watch when they were doing those things.

(*When they were shooting?*) Yes. And then they said to us: "Look, when you are not doing what we tell you, you'll be next." This was their way of telling us. But the people they were shooting were usually people from outside. Sometimes we knew where they came from, but sometimes we didn't; they were different kinds of people. Anyway, then we went back to work. You see, these were the conditions we were working in there.

The laundry room

After this work, they sent us to the washing rooms. This is really… You wouldn't believe this story. This shows you how we were helping each other. We had such a big—how you call that, you know the place where many women wash together?

(*Laundry room?*) Yes, this was the laundry room. There was like a tub, very long. We each washed, mostly linen, clothes, very bloody ones, and we were washing the bloody things in cold water, and this was winter. I want to tell you that when I was washing there, this was again a good cold job. I had such an infection in my leg from standing in this wet constantly that till today I have places that you can see with holes. There was a hole big enough to put a finger in. I would run an infection. The pus from it was like a string, so bad it was, a really open hole. They took me one day to some kind of clinic, but that didn't help, because I went back to the same kind of work.

Then when we were washing, the guys who went out to work, they didn't have a chance to clean their clothes. We took their clothes from them to wash. And they paid us again the same way, money or bread. But how could we bring this stuff in, and how could they take this stuff out? Covering it up wasn't bad, because the Germans didn't come very often to the laundry room. Sometimes, right away we would say to them, "We'll cover your pieces with what we wash for the

Germans. But when we finish washing, you have to dry those things." This was mostly shirts, men's shirts. Other Jewish women were working in a drying place. Drying wasn't like today's drying machines. They were hanging the clothes up to dry. Then part of my money—let's say they gave me five dollars for the shirts, part of this five dollars I gave a woman to dry the shirt for me. This was not all. Part of the money I had to give to another one who was ironing the shirts.

These were the shirts for the guys who went out to work. Every day I'd take the shirts. Evenings when they came from work, I could go to the barracks, and they'd give them to me. The Germans didn't know. They could think we were their wives, washing them in the latrine when we washed ourselves. And to bring them in, we put them all on us. We were all thin and malnourished. And we put all those shirts around us, five shirts, six shirts, and covered them with our jackets, and this is the way we went to work. Then we took them off and put them in the water together with the German clothes. When we finished with the wash, we gave them to the women who did the drying. Then we went to the women who ironed. Now we had a package of ironed clothes, a nice package. How did we take them out from the laundry? There were women working night shifts and day shifts. So we had to make a kind of association together. When I was working in the daytime, the woman who was working the night shift came under the window at a certain time when she knew that I was going to throw the package through the window.

Does this sound funny to you? It wasn't funny to us, always looking to make sure that nobody saw us doing this job, because later it was so tough that we couldn't do even that. You know what I said before, that they weren't paying attention? After they found out about those packages, nobody wanted to say who the people were who did it. They called us to the *Appellplatz* [the central place where they did roll calls several times a day] and beat twenty to fifty people to get them to say who was doing that. And nobody would say anything, even though we were beaten like I cannot tell you how.

Then we had to find a different way to take these things out from the laundry room. We put the wet things on ourselves, you see, because we knew we had no way to dry and iron, because the packages could not go through the window. We put the wet stuff around us and went to the barracks, and then the woman who had another shift, day or night, she dried the things outside and ironed them in the barracks. You see, this was a new system we had invented. And this way they didn't say anything, because they wanted us to keep clean, and they wanted us to wash and iron. I am telling you, from the moment when we were putting those wet things around us, with the jackets on the top to go out with the wet clothes to the barracks, all of us had to watch. When the package went through the window, five people had to watch. One was in the doorway, one in the window, one on the outside, then nobody saw the old person who came to catch the package. I don't know if the Germans knew what kind of work was done in between work there. And this, you see, that's how—this is the way we had some food and some money.

(*Were there leaders within the camp?*) Sure. They called them *Kapo*. There was a big leader who was Jewish. I forget his name. My girlfriend in New York would remember because he was a good friend of her brother's. You saw the movie about Schindler and the people who worked in his factory?

(*You knew about that?*) Yes, people who had money could go there. People without money couldn't go there. Or people who had something they knew how to do, business or something that he needed, Schindler took them. And my girlfriend's brother had a chance because of the Jewish guy working for Goeth. Goeth was very smart, that German. He said, "When I make one Jew the big one, he can go and do for me whatever I need." Paulleck, I think, was his first name. The second name I can't remember. He had a wife and a few more people in his family. Anyway, Goeth killed them all near the end. He put the whole family in the center of the place and killed one after the other.

(*Who did this?*) That Goeth. All this time, the guy who was thinking he'd survive, he'd be—I don't know who, Goeth showed us near the end. "Look what I have done with him."

(*Why did he do that?*) This we cannot know. Maybe he was afraid. It was near the time to close this camp to go to another camp. Maybe he was afraid somebody would find out what he was giving Paulleck. Because I heard Goeth gave Paulleck money and jewelry, whatever, and Paulleck was thinking that one day he would survive. He didn't. But he wasn't bad. He gave money to the people from Schindler's factory for my girlfriend's brother. My girlfriend's brother said, "I don't want to take the money from you." But Paullek didn't listen to him. He gave the money to Schindler's people anyway, and they took him to the factory to work, and he survived. He is in Australia. He survived because of Schindler. They took him because this bad guy, the Jew, gave them money. He arranged that they took him there.

I don't know if I told you about this moment when the Germans said they were going to take everything from us. Money, jewelry, everything. I was on the bed sleeping with this woman whose husband was working in leather, and she had everything. She never asked me if I maybe wanted a little bit of soup or maybe wanted a little bit of bread, never. She's alive in Canada. She's very well off. She married one of the guys who was working in this factory. He was on the machine there, and now he has a factory in Canada making sweaters. This mean German taught him something. And when they said they had come to take our money and jewelry, I said, "Look, I have so little that I have to put it someplace in our cover or something, because if they take it from me, I cannot survive."

She said, "No way you are going to leave money or anything here, because I don't want to be killed."

I told her, "Look, it's easy for you. You have a husband who works and brings you stuff. Nobody brings me anything."

She said, "I am going to tell the Germans what you don't tell them." I gave it away; I gave them all away because, you see, I had no choice. I'm just telling you what the circumstances were. I am sure if she maybe one day reads my book—I don't mention her name, but she knows who she is. She would be aggravated that I am talking about her. I think I have the right, because she really could have helped me, and she could have said she didn't know that I did that. This was my risk. She said, "Not in our cover, no way." There was no other place to put the money or the little jewelry that I had.

A few days later, they called us and said they needed women to separate diamonds, other stones and gold, and money. They chose women in the line who were going to do that, and this is again my story. I could be a very rich woman, because when they did that, the women had another idea. Then, we still had hair. They cut our hair later, in Auschwitz. They were putting the money and jewels in their hair, and no one was looking inside it. When they were choosing those women, I ran away again. Why? I heard that every day after sorting those things, you had to parade naked in front of the Germans, and they looked all over your body to see if you were hiding diamonds. I was thinking, I'd rather die. I couldn't see myself parading in this way. Then I ran away. After I saw what happened, I was sorry. I don't know if I would do the same thing again, but I was sorry that I didn't do it.

(*They were still able to hide things?*) You see, they were going to the latrine during this time. They put it inside the latrine, in the *Wascherei*. They were attaching those things to the hole in the latrine, and somebody else took them from there. They had a lot of diamonds and gold and things like that. Some of these women came to Auschwitz. This was the last transport, so late that even in Auschwitz they didn't have time to look at them, because the Russians came right away and then the English Army came and liberated us. Those women kept this jewelry.

(*How long were you in this camp altogether?*) You know, I cannot tell you exactly. I think I was there about one year. From there I went to Auschwitz. I cannot tell you exactly. After Auschwitz was the worst, Bergen-Belsen. There was really nothing, nothing to eat.

Appellplatz

When I was working in this washroom, one day there came some news that there would be a big *Appell* [roll call]. They asked everybody to come to one place. You wouldn't believe it. They played beautiful music, and they were taking all the kids—there were kids there—to Auschwitz, and they were beating the mothers that didn't want to bring their kids to the wagon. And the Appell, usually that's where they were beating people every day, ten people, twenty-five, you know. We would stand there, and they would come and beat one; this was the way they got to your brain. And the music played a beautiful song. And you stayed there, and they beat you.

One day when I was in the *Wascherei*, the news came that there would be a big Appell for everybody and that they were going to choose people to send to Auschwitz to be shot. They had done that a few times just to show us so we didn't think this life was too good for us, to make us on guard and see what was going to happen to us anyway. And we had a Kapo, a German Kapo. I don't know if he was half German, but he wasn't Jewish. And he heard about what was going to happen at the roll call and in this washroom there was a shelf but this wasn't a normal shelf. You can imagine, they put all those big bags there from the army, dirty stuff and bloody stuff, and the shelf was large like a door, such a big shelf. When he heard about the Appell he told us—I don't remember how many we were, but we were enough to fit on the shelf. He told us to go on the shelf and lie down there in the back of it. He put all the dirty laundry in the front, and we were staying there through the whole Appell, on the shelf, the people from the washing rooms. What I heard when we came out, you wouldn't believe it. This was one of the worst days in Krakow-Plaszöw—from the Appell. They were shooting and beating, and it was terrible. And we said to ourselves, "We are OK; we are hiding in the washroom, and he has done that for us." Because you never heard about those things, that there was somebody who could do that. OK, he was thinking he was not in danger, because he could always say we had done that by ourselves.

I didn't know that he went to the Appellplatz and said, "I am sure those people (us) went out." But it was his idea for us to do that, because he heard it would be very bad. You know, news about what would happen always came from the house, our commander, the big shot. You see, there were Jewish Kapo too, good ones and bad ones. Germans made them Kapo to help them find things out from us, to help do bad things to us, but some of them couldn't do it. They were acting like they were working for the Germans, but they were really helping us.

There was a big warehouse with all the clothes, the striped clothes we were wearing, and there were other things like blankets that they took from the people who came in from Krakow. It was winter, and I didn't have anything to wear, and I went to those warehouses and told them I didn't have a blanket. You see, there it wasn't as bad as in Auschwitz. If you didn't have a blanket, they would give you an extra blanket. And they gave me one blanket. I'll never forget this blanket; this was such a nice brown blanket with stripes. Those things that they gave us to wear, that jacket was very thin. It was winter, it was cold, so I figured out that I was going to make a skirt and wear it under this jacket so I'd be warm. One day I put this skirt on, and a girl came and started screaming. She said, "You cut my blanket!"

I said, "What do you mean, I cut your blanket? They gave me the blanket in the warehouse where they keep all those things." She insisted this was her blanket. And she was all ready to go to the Kapo and tell him. Then I said, "OK, take this skirt. It's your skirt. I cannot bring the blanket back." Now I never forget this.

(*And she took it?*) Sure she took it, why not? This wasn't really hers, because the Germans took it from her and gave it to me. They gave me the blanket, and I made this skirt.

But she said this was hers. What was I going to do? I was going to wait until she went and told them I cut the blanket, and then who knows what? So I gave her the skirt. Such a small thing, but you cannot forget in your life what happened.

There was a Jewish Kapo in Plaszöw who helped us too. He was working for the Germans, but he was helping when he was working in the warehouse. He gave us things. I was talking with people after the war about who was a good Kapo, who was a bad Kapo. He was a really good Kapo. He helped us in many things, and you see, you hear different things in the camp, and you don't know what is really true. This is just like in normal life— you hear something, and you don't know. It could be the press, could be the newspaper, and sometimes there were those kinds of stories then. We didn't know whether to believe it or not to believe it, but you know, there were many things that we didn't believe, that were true. Like all those stories that they were building the crematoriums all over the place and that we would be ending up there—that we'd go in there too. We'd hear things like that. Even when I heard that before going to Krakow-Plaszöw, I didn't believe it. Who could think this would be possible? In the beginning they were just burning bodies and putting their remains in the earth.

One time I was in the latrine with my friend. We saw a package there. I said to her, "Don't touch it. We'll go out and see what it is in the barracks." We went out, and she was already afraid, because, you know, when you have something on you that is not kosher, you think everybody will see that. And we came to the barracks, and she opened it. There was money sewed all around, and she took the money and said, "Now we are going to live." We went to the barracks to the guys who came from work. I'll never forget, we were so hungry. This was the worst time. It was tough for guys to bring the bread. I don't know how they could bring flour in. Probably they managed to do it with the soldiers. I don't know so much about that, because I wasn't going out and in, but they were bringing in flour. We were mixing it with water and making like a pancake. Each barrack had a stove—not a stove to cook on, a stove to heat. There were a few of them with such a round top like an old-fashioned kind. There was no chimney; this was like a stove which heated the room. On top of that, we were cleaning and mixing this flour with water, these pancakes. I'll never forget when we poured the flour and we were doing those pancakes. This was luxury. You see, with this water soup, to have those pancakes, this was luxury. And this money went for these pancakes. Also we bought candy; this was the same money. We went around to try to sell it, but we couldn't. So we ate the candy, and this was one of the things that I also can never forget. I was a bad seller. I couldn't sell the candy, so I ate it myself.

The moment my friend found the money in the latrine, this was something like—we said that this came from God. I don't recall exactly, but I think I didn't work anymore in *Strickerei*, in this factory with tricots. Whatever I was doing, I couldn't make any money there. Then we were sorting things, but the way they were watching us, we couldn't do anything anymore with those pieces. Really, we didn't have money, and this was—we said, "This money came from God." You know, you would never have expected it. Always, this was one thing on your mind—eating. Yes, eating.

After the war, I kept thinking I was fat and thin and fat and thin. My husband's friend was a doctor. He was Julian's best friend. They went together to the Sorbonne; he studied medicine, Julian studied aviation. I was his patient. They called me a miracle. One day he said, "What is going on with you?"

I told him, "When I have a day when I'm thinking about the camp, then I may be hungry again. Then I start to eat, I get fat, then I hate myself and I stop eating." My stomach was like a sponge—fat and thin and fat and thin. I have always had a problem with my stomach from the concentration camp till today. This hiatus hernia does things in my stomach so that I always have acidity. This is from the concentration camp. If something is bothering me, I don't eat.

You know, many men in there, they would come to our barracks proposing we do things, then they'd give us money. (*These were Jews or Germans?*) Jews, Jews. German, they wouldn't dare. Germans did sexual things, but I never was in contact with that. I know they did, because I knew one woman who was going with a German, and she got very much from him. It really never happened to me. You see, I cannot tell you about…I knew there were things like that. Yes, Jewish people, Jewish people. I don't know today if I would see it differently. Then, I was a young woman; I was disgusted. You know, today you understand what the problem is. We all were thinking we wouldn't survive, and like they say, men have a stronger urge than women. This may not have been true, because we were more occupied with feeding ourselves. These were the men who were going to work, giving us those shirts. I knew some of them. One man said, "Mirka, why you should wash and go after the money in such a hard way? You can have easy money (having sex with him)." I said, "No, this is not easy money for me." And after the war, you might think I was stupid.

(*Did your friends do that?*) Yes. Ach. Evening in the barracks, under the barracks, what are you talking about? It happened all the time. And there was one woman, a Kapo. She's alive; she lives in Israel. I am not going to mention her name. She had every night another guy. And it was normal, was normal. I remember that one time, that was a terrible shock for me. In Auschwitz in the morning, they were bringing us coffee—really this was brown hot water. We were in this Mustard camp, you know, Auschwitz—I say, "Mustard macht frei." ["Arbeiten Macht Frei" (Work sets you free) was the notorious sign over the entrance of Auschwitz. Miriam substituted "mustard" for "work" since they gave them plates of mustard at Auschwitz.] Special to show the dignitaries, they were bringing us coffee, and we were supposed to take this big thing with coffee to give back to the woman after it was empty. Every time, another one of us took care of that. And one day I went with my girl-friend with the coffee pot and one of these guys attacked me—completely attacked me, and I said, "Go away from me, or you know what," and he said, "Don't worry, I am not a man anymore." I'll never forget that. This was a shock for me. I didn't realize what he really meant—he's not a man anymore. Afterward I found out about these things that the Germans had done in the laboratory; they were, you know, cutting, castrating men.

4 Birkenau and Auschwitz

I was in the Krakow Plaszöw camp maybe six months, maybe a little bit longer, and they started talking about transportation from this camp to another camp. I was lucky, they took me from Plaszöw to Auschwitz. Lucky people went from Plaszöw, this was the best thing, to Auschwitz. We were women, young women, looking well, so they took us. In the beginning I was in mustard camp. They dressed us up to make like a show camp.

Everybody went first to Birkenau. After that, they were sending people to different places. The first night when we came there, they put us, the ones that he chose to live, in the barracks, you know. But before they put us in the barracks, they gave us uniforms. They took all our stuff. They sent us to Mengele. He decided who went left, who went right. They took old people right away to kill them; all us young people he put to work. We were there, I don't know, maybe three weeks. You're not allowed to be sick; no, we gave sickness to others. It was winter. We had such thin clothes, jackets and pants with those stripes. We were wearing skirts also with the stripes, and nothing else underneath. It was winter; we would shiver.

They took us to this laundry place to wash ourselves, and they gave us those uniforms. Then we saw the hundreds and hundreds of fur coats and shoes, and there was a Jewish couple working there. This couple, I don't know, they say they were doing it for some time, and then they took them to the oven. This I cannot tell you for sure, because we didn't have a chance to talk with these people. We went just once through, and that's all. This was near the oven. When we were going out, there were piles and piles of coats and dresses, suits, shoes, you know—they took everything. And suddenly I saw on the pile of clothes some big coat with the Jewish yellow star. I grabbed this coat with me. I don't know if this was intuition—I don't know why. The Germans could have killed me. They didn't look; they said, "Let her go." I went.

It was a very good idea because we didn't have too many blankets. This was a tremendous coat. This must have been from a very big man, fat and tall. Every night they called us to the Appell. Three o'clock at night, four o'clock at night, Germans wanted girls to go from the barracks and stay for two hours, three hours, and it was winter. I had the big coat, and I was standing always—we were four, but I was standing like one. All my girlfriends, three in front of me, were covered with this coat. Can you imagine how big that was?

(*You must have been very popular.*) Not that. I was always fast thinking, you see. I survived the war because of fast thinking. Because I was in many spots when I had to run or cover myself, things like that. We were covered. Usually it was dark, and the Germans didn't look so close. They wanted us just to stand there frozen—to freeze I mean. We were never talking much about the coat we got, but somehow we were in this coat, and we weren't freezing very much. This I cannot forget. This is something that will really stay with me—the big brown coat with the big yellow star.

We were there three weeks. During the three weeks, one day they called us, and they started to do these numbers. You know, this machine. Each thing, like the letter or number, had a hundred points with an electric needle.

(*Did it hurt?*) I don't know. You don't feel hurting in the position you are in. You don't have enough to eat. You know, the whole situation. There was one—such a big pail that everybody went to. Later there was a latrine, but in the time when we were there, it was the pail. It was terrible—everyone had to take that out every morning. Anyway, they called us for this putting on the numbers. And we were standing in the line, and they put on the numbers. After they put on the numbers, a German officer came, and he started to look at our hands. We didn't know why he was looking at our hands, and he put a few women on the side. I was among them. I said, "Uh oh"; you have to laugh—right away it came to my mind, "Run away." This was all the time from the moment the Germans came to Poland. You know, when I was on the street, if I saw a few of them, I knew I had to go into a house before I went near them or turn the corner to not go near them. You see, I didn't look Jewish, but they started to come and ask for things and papers. I had the papers because I was working legally. Then you were scared, but you couldn't show you were scared, because this would…My father played poker, and he always was winning. My mother was very mad at him. She said, "Win in somebody else's house, not in our own house." He said, "I cannot help it." I learned from my father to look after myself. I learned with the Germans not to show them that I was scared. I could die inside me. You learn the hard way. It was part of my father's poker game, the way he was managing.

When the Germans put us, a few women, on the other side, I was thinking, "What was it he saw in my hands?" During the war when they were bombarding Poland, Lodz, I started to chew my nails, and my father said, "Please don't do it." Because when I was young—now you don't see—I had really nice hands, long fingers, and my father said, "Please don't do that. Save your hands." This was in my father's family, those long fingers. He gave me cigarettes. This was the beginning of my smoking. Later the Germans gave us—they didn't give you food, but they gave you cigarettes and mustard. A plate with mustard, can you believe that? How much you want it. You can eat mustard? We ate mustard. And this came to my mind because I was scared to death. I was thinking I had to run, after this, when they put numbers on our arms, forearms. And I ran away. You don't know when to run and when not to run. You know, women who were so scared they were standing— paralyzed in place—sometimes my feet are always like inside and you cannot move. This happened to you in the circumstances there.

But this time, somehow, I slid out. I ran. And then I found out later that those women went to Czechoslovakia. He was looking for women with long fingers to make bulbs in a factory. They needed long fingers to put some kind of wire in, and this was the reason. And they had a good life; they were sleeping well and eating well, and they survived the war. When I think now—you see, I am not religious; I believe in God. I think God wanted me to survive. Because I saw I had nine lives during my time in the concentration camps. I had so many times to make decisions to do or not to do. Now I see this was God telling me to do it, to survive. Sometimes when I ran away, it was nonsense, but I didn't realize that. This was the first time that happened, but I found out, a long time later, where the women went because two of them I knew well. I met them after the war. In fact, I met them in Sweden in the sanatorium. I ran away that time. Afterward when I found out what happened, I thought how stupid I was. But you cannot always be smart.

In Auschwitz the bathing house was terrible. They gave us some kind of water. This Sunday my friend in New York called. I was with her in the concentration camp for a long time. I met her there. This was really some meeting. I was working in the laundry. In the laundry, you know, you had a lot of towels and pieces of soap and things like that. Other people who weren't in the laundry couldn't have that in the concentration camp. I remember we were in the latrine. I was washing myself as she stood near me. She said, "Oh I would give, I don't know what, to have soap." I said, "Go ahead, wash yourself with it." This was our meeting. This woman would never be my friend in normal times in Poland. We were completely from different kinds of families, you see. We would have had nothing to do with each other. But we are friends from the concentration camp now.

(*What kind of family was she from?*) Very religious, very poor, not educated. Really, I would have had nothing to do with her. My father wasn't that old. He made such jokes, you know, on Yom Kippur, the day when people can't eat. He joked that he couldn't go to restaurants to eat pork. Father joked. My mother was very mad when he was talking like that because my mother was—not religious but the holidays were for her very important, and she made us grow up like that. On Yom Kippur I came to eat; she let us eat. She said, "You are kids." In the kitchen there was always something to eat because we always had a servant who wasn't Jewish. But she didn't want to see us eating in the main part of the house. She said, "Go to the kitchen to eat."

She spent all Yom Kippur in synagogue. Father had to go and take her home in the evening, but she didn't take us. She didn't want it put on us; she left us the way we were. If we felt like going, then we went. I don't know if that was right. I think I made George more Jewish than my mother made me. Maybe the concentration camp has done that. We saw then what happened to Jews. So when George was small, I sent him to Sunday school, to synagogue, and I felt that George was more Jewish than me until he died. I felt he should grow up knowing about what happened, and he was very much interested. And not just that, he had feelings about all those millions of Holocaust victims. He was in the second generation group, kids of people from the Holocaust. He was very active in that. Maybe being in that group with them made him feel strongly about what we suffered. He was nice, caring, because he knew we had lost everybody. He was our only son. This is the reason it's harder [that he died at a relatively young age]. We were in school where we learned everything, but this was really a Christian school, because you had crosses on the wall. But there were religion classes. We had a rabbi who came to teach us. We always left the class because we were—let's just say that in a class of forty girls, there were maybe ten Jewish girls. Then we always left the class and we went for our religion class…But this wasn't religion really. He taught Jewish history. This wasn't religion. I never took Hebrew. Julian, yes.

Many things I should have told you before. Now, I said that when I came to Birkenau, Mengele, he was putting us in groups of who goes to live and who goes to be burned. We already knew these things. Because when we were in the small town, Dzialoszyce, we ran away from the ghetto. We didn't want to go to the ghetto. My father gave the idea to my mother, like those two cousins who are in Australia because they ran to Russia when Hitler came, just before Hitler came. We knew he was coming to Poland. Things first started when he threw all Polish-born people who were living in Germany to Auschwitz in Poland. He put them on the frontier. I don't know if I told you, but my mother came to us and said, "Hitler has thrown away Jews from Germany. And you girls have to look for things. I want to send packages to those people." I remember me with Lonya, my sister; we were talking about what we were supposed to give to the people. We made packages, and my mother sent them to a special organization for sending them on, because Hitler didn't let people with suitcases go from Germany to Poland. What I tried to tell you earlier, we were very moved, but this was a shirt. This was like something on us that we felt, but it wasn't us. We tried to give them, to send to them, but it wasn't us. We knew we suffered because we were Jews—but when we were in the camps ourselves it was like skin. This is my comparison, between shirts and skin.

(*You were eighteen.*) I was a little bit older. You think you have to run. This was in my head always: "Run. Just save yourself." Now when I think why I went through all that, for what? I wanted to survive the war so much you wouldn't believe. I ran away to survive the war, and now I say, "For what?"

(If you hadn't survived, you wouldn't ever have had George.)
Yes, but I don't have him.

(But you had him for a long time. Just at that moment, just during the war, you wanted to get through that point of time.)

When we were in the small city, in Dzialoszyce, my father was a very tall, handsome-looking guy. And they—mostly, the Jewish people in this town, they were small guys. I remember him. There was a place at the market when the Germans weren't there. They were standing talking politics, you know, and he always said, I heard him, "I have to survive the war. I have to survive the war." And this was in my head, you know. I felt I had to survive the war. And maybe this was the reason I really was strong, to tell myself, "I have to do it. I have to do it."

Now, I don't know if you know. Birkenau was on the side. Near Auschwitz was a big door and the sign "Arbeit Macht Frei" (Work makes you free), and they chose girls, young and healthy-looking, to go there. Why? Because this was the place where dignitaries came from different countries to see how we lived there because Hitler said we had a good life really. It was very clean inside. We had clean bunks, they changed our laundry every week and blankets, and we got coffee in the morning, and a portion of margarine, bread, and sausage every evening. When dignitaries came from another country, they showed us off to see how good the prisoners really had it in the camp. Outside the camp they didn't show, because we went from the camp and were carrying bricks, cutting the grass, and carrying those pieces to irrigate the water and things like that. When you weren't working that fast, they beat you and this kind of thing. Every day they were bringing people to the camp, and then we already knew what was really happening— they were burning the corpses. And to survive, you had to work, do what they wanted, because we didn't know anyway how long we'd be able to survive.

This was not long, but we were working like horses. You know, they make this—what do you call that in English—irrigation? When you want to put water out? We were digging ditches; we were carrying pieces of grass with the dirt to put on another place to stop the water going the way they didn't want it. This wasn't work to work; this was work just to make us work like horses. We were carrying bricks. What can I tell you; this was work for nothing. First we were working, and two girls were carrying the soup that we were supposed to eat in the middle of the day, just really watered soup. Then they made us carry those things, bricks and pieces of grass and dirt and things like that. This wasn't worth doing. This was how we worked. Out from the barracks to this work and back for the night. Then when we were coming in at night, I don't remember exactly—they gave us the morning or evening to read. Anyway, in the morning we had coffee, bad coffee always, and cigarettes and mustard. I'll never forget that. Anyway we were hungry, terribly hungry.

This was not a long time that we were in this Auschwitz. What was really something was that you could still live. We didn't know that Hitler ordered that they put something in our food. We were just surprised that everybody had lost her menstruation; we didn't realize why. Afterward we found out what this was: they put something in our wheat that we ate, and whatever they gave us we ate because we were hungry, then we stopped menstruating. This was in Auschwitz.

(*So you knew people were being killed?*) Sure, we knew that. We knew even before; my father mentioned it. We didn't know then, but I found out when I was in Rava-Ruska that they were burning people. But it wasn't the same system. In Auschwitz they chose another system with burning. The people weren't supposed to know they were going to be burned. They told them they were going to wash themselves, and they never came out because gas was there. And then there were special people, Kapo; this was mostly Jewish or other—Gypsy or I don't know, who took the corpses from there and put them in the grave or burned them. When you went there, inside, you saw those rooms with shoes, rooms with coats, a room with keys—they took all the gold from them. We were like mummies then; but after, when you remember all those things...Glasses, the room with glasses, you wouldn't believe it.

(*What did you talk about, among yourselves?*) Just how to survive. How to survive, where we should go, not go, how we could run away or something. You see, those bunks (*prycza*) in the barracks. You believe this was like pieces of wood? You put six or seven, and this was the bed. Sometimes you came in and there was a hole; someone would steal our things. You see, we were looking for people who we knew would be staying in the barracks during the day, then they could look out for that, and when we came back at night, we looked out for them. Bergen Belsen was even worse.

One day we were sitting, waiting to be burned because somebody said, "It is your turn." And we were sitting there, and then came the German officer. He said, "I need young girls to work," and he chose us. Like I always say, I have nine lives. So many times I was ready to be burned or this or that. We were there a long time, every day, and you couldn't know what they expected. There were fighting people, shouting people, and they came sometimes with full vans with kids, and you knew they were taking them to be burned.

The Appellplatz was the worst thing. They put on music, beautiful music, American singers, beautiful melodies. And the singer was singing, music was playing, and they were shooting. Such irony, nobody would believe it could be done in such a circumstance. After this terrible thing, we knew that every day the transport came, people were going straight to the crematorium. You ask what were we talking about, we were just thinking, "Maybe I can get out there; maybe I'll survive the war." My thinking was always, "I have to survive. I have to survive. I have…" Maybe that's why I ran away from many things, because I was thinking, "Maybe this beats death."

One day they said to us—they didn't tell us, no, we heard,—that the Russians were approaching. And then we knew because suddenly they were giving us big portions of bread and jam and sausage, and we didn't know what happened, and they said, "Now we are moving you to another camp." They didn't know what to do with all those supplies so they gave them to us, and we carried them. This was a big walk [a death march]. From Auschwitz we went to Bergen Belsen. Partly we went on the open trucks and partly walking. I remember when it was night and we were walking. They told us we could sleep in barns and places like that. Some of my friends were staying. They said, "We are not going; we are just staying here. I said, "What happens to you when the Russians come? They'll kill you." They said, "No, they won't kill us. We'll be OK." I heard later that the Russians were raping women; it wasn't OK for those who stayed. Nothing was OK then.

5 Bergen Belsen

(*How far was it from Auschwitz to Bergen Belsen?*) I really don't recall. I know it was a few days of traveling. [It's 47 miles.] Bergen Belsen was a murder camp. There was nothing to eat. Dirt. The Kapo were Russian. You see, in Auschwitz you had many Kapo who were Jewish and even Polish, but here were just Russians and bad Russian women; they were hurting us. When Hitler went to Russia, they sent many Russian people to the camps to punish them. They gave us pieces of bread to buy shoes. I was just wearing rags on my feet, but I never could buy the shoes. We walked in snow.

The Russians were prisoners too, but the Germans gave them privileges because they were strong. We were already in the camp so long that we were like animals. They pushed us, we were dead. They were very strong. Russian people were strong. Jews were strong. My mother was a strong woman, my father too. I never recall him being sick. Once he had an infection in his arm. This is one thing I remember about my father. My other memory is that he was so strong he was swimming in icy water.

The Russians, they weren't Jewish. They were so strong, so the Germans made them Kapo. And that was terrible. There wasn't work. We were dying from hunger. Most everybody had typhoid fever and stomach sickness. And in the end, I couldn't even walk. This was a miracle when the English Army came to Bergen-Belsen [April 15, 1945]. Before that, I have to tell you, this was—we knew that every day, every night, this was like three, four o'clock in the afternoon, they came for people to go peel potatoes, peel cabbages, all those things which went to the … I really don't know who was eating those things they were cooking there. And this was a fight. You imagine? We were fighting to be able to go to the kitchen to peel potatoes because we could eat the raw potatoes. One woman was helping another this way. When the Germans came, there were maybe a hundred or more people who wanted to go to the kitchen. Then they were beating us. Then we gave up, and they had just the number they needed. This was a big entrance, no door, and we went through it with the German soldier to the kitchen. I'll never forget the way they were beating us to separate us so they didn't have too many people to go there, and this was a fight every morning to be able to go to eat these raw potatoes to survive. They wanted fewer people to go, and they didn't know how to do it. When they were beating us, they knew—and this was true—that many people would give up.

Also, we didn't sleep at night, to be able to go very early to be in the front of the entrance. I was sick after coming to Bergen-Belsen. I had some gloves that they gave us, with one finger, like you have for skiing, one finger. And they were so big that on the end of the glove I could put in a few flat potatoes, then I wrapped the glove tight with some rags. I knew there were hungry people in the barracks, so every day I put a few flat potatoes in this glove. We went out from the kitchen, and they were always looking at us, touching us, but they never came to the gloves. I would be dead, for sure. I was bringing the people those potatoes to the barracks. We were eating the potatoes there, the raw potatoes. This was one thing we could survive on for the time being. And this was a few months, and you know, people started to be cannibals. They were starting to eat themselves. It was terrible. This was the worst thing.

Why did I have to bring the potatoes? Because there were sick people. I just asked them to keep my pieces of potato because when I came from work, they would be stolen. A few women were always there on the upper bunks then. They were beaten, and I tell you, it was a terrible place to be, worse than everything else. And those Russian Kapo were terrible. We were supposed to get some water soup in the evening, but we wouldn't get it. We were just starving until we were dead. And those women, I brought them potatoes, and they were keeping an eye on my things. I gave them all those pieces, and when I came down I could sleep there. And this was like that for a few months. Then I was sick, so I couldn't go to the kitchen. I went to the barracks. I remember one woman had such a small bag with sugar, and when I was lying there sick, she took some on her finger and put it on my tongue. She said, "Have a little bit of sugar."

One day we saw Germans with white flags going away in cars, and you wouldn't believe it. This was the day when our Kapo started cleaning. It meant that all the women who were up on the beds sick had to go out from the barracks. We said, "Where should we go?" They said, "We don't care." Then we lay under the barracks. We didn't have any choice what to do. This was with my two friends from Krakow. And I couldn't walk there. I went on my hands from the barracks to this place because I already had typhoid fever. We were under the barracks. Suddenly we heard Russian women screaming, "Nazi idiot, this means our people are coming." She said, "Our army is coming." And we saw no Russians. She was thinking the Russians had come, but it was the English Army.

You see, Julian was lucky; he was in a concentration camp for just six months. When the Russians came, he was sick. He couldn't walk. A Russian took care of him. They sent him to Russia to a hospital, and from there they sent him back to Marseilles, to France. It was lucky he was sick. He didn't go through what I did. He didn't care that he was sick. He said, "When the Russians come, they will kill me," but they didn't kill the men, they just raped the woman, or some were lucky and nothing happened.

But then when that happened, my girlfriend told me, "You heard?" I said, "What?" She said, "You didn't hear?" And the English soldiers came. They took us from under the barracks; they took us away from there, because this was a death camp. The smell, this was just people lying, you know, dead people, one on top of another. They took us to the places where the Germans who ran away lived, in their houses, in the army barracks, where there was real luxury, and they put us there. I was feeling like I was dying. I remember one soldier came and asked us what we wanted. I had such a feeling in my stomach. I said I need something acidic, and he brought me apples. I couldn't eat those apples, and we all had diarrhea. They didn't know why. One captain came, an officer. He said, "I don't under-stand what's going on. You people are starving, and there are thousands of loaves of bread on the truck. Why didn't they give them to you?"

Then one soldier was very smart. He said, "You know what, before we give that to them to eat, let us check." And they had brought dogs and cats with them in the helicop-ters, and they gave them the bread. You know what? There was glass in the bread, it was glass that looked like flour. They baked the bread with that flour. They were thinking they were going to have time. If the British had given all the people in the concentration camp the bread, we would have died because our stomach insides would be completely cut. We found out the Germans had given that to us even before in the other camp, a little bit of that, and this was the reason why we had stomach problems, diarrhea, and all those things afterward. But this was luck that somebody said, "Let's check it," because otherwise we would be dead, all of us.

And it took time until they could bring food with planes, with helicopters, and they were throwing it away because most of us couldn't eat. Our stomachs were completely shrunken, and when I asked for this apple, you know, I was chewing, and I was keeping it in my mouth for hours. I remember one soldier came with dresses. He gave me a dress that had a very small waist. I didn't think I could fit into it. I said, "This is no dress for me."

He said, "You don't see yourself; you'd better try." I tried on the dress, but we still had those fleas on us. They had to put us in another barracks and take all the things and burn them, and this was terrible.

I felt so happy when the British came. The happiness was how a very sick person would feel when he could walk again. I didn't know if I'd be able to walk again. When we were in the barracks, one day I said, "I will die during the night." And one girl, she was very religious, she started praying for me. I don't know why, but I felt like I was seeing death, you know. I saw something white was coming to me while she was praying.

You know, we were so sick there. We were so thankful to the English army. We didn't know what would happen to us after such a long time under the Germans. Then we heard that people in Sweden wanted to help us in the camp, to take us away, and this happened the day after I said, "I feel like I am going to die." I was so weak I couldn't even eat, couldn't move, nothing. I was just bones. Then I started seeing the other girls. I saw that most of them looked like me. We didn't look at each other before, you know; we had those striped jackets. A few days later, people from Sweden came, and they asked us if we wanted to go there. They said that we were going to have a good life and that they would give us everything we needed, doctors and two sanatoriums. I don't remember exactly, but we had some kind of examination; the really sick ones went first. They found out I couldn't walk, I had diarrhea, and I couldn't eat. I also had tuberculosis. I was on the first transport to Sweden.

6 The End of the War

Sweden

I cannot tell you what the Swedish people have done for us. They were treating us like princes. They had carriages to take us to have a bath. We started with milk, because the doctor explained that he wanted our stomachs to open; they were completely shrunken. The milk changed into something like cheese. Things that I remember, this is funny—the nurse came to ask us what we wanted. No, first of all they gave us milk, however much we wanted. We were drinking and drinking and drinking. I needed something sour. So I put the milk under my night table to make buttermilk. Buttermilk is sour. I knew what they did in Poland when I was a child. My father always ate it a lot. I always took off the cream from the top of the milk and ate that. One day the nurse caught me. She said, "What are you eating?"

I said, "This buttermilk." She said, "You shouldn't have that; you should have the milk."

I said, "I need something sour," and she said I had to wait. And they brought us bread. I'll never forget that. Plates with bread, bread without stopping. We couldn't finish eating. I had so many bones. I couldn't sit even. I had to have a pillow to be able to sit. And then I started to walk a little bit with two nurses walking with me. I couldn't walk by myself.

In Sweden, first of all, we were in Linköping. We were in a sanatorium. They gave us medicine, and we went to the doctor. In the best circumstances you could have—no matter how rich you were, you could not find what they did for us in Sweden. The *Oberdoctor* [top doctor], the biggest shot, he was sitting with the magnifying glasses when they gave us permission to walk. They had us on the list. They could tell if you were walking longer than you were supposed to walk. You wouldn't imagine, one day they opened the door, and there were coats, dresses, shoes, everything you needed, brassiere and panties; you could choose color and size. I cannot tell you all that they had done for us. For us, this was like a miracle.

And then they started to send us to different clinics. I remember one girl who had pleurisy, water in the lungs, and she said, "They gave us a treatment for cleaning water out of the lungs. They were putting air into our lungs with a machine." She said this really was no good, after the treatment they were sicker. I don't know what was the reason for that. One day they called me to the doctor's office and said I needed that treatment. After hearing what she said, I ran away. This was my running away still from the concentration camp. I said, "I don't want to be more sick." Whatever I was feeling, I thought I could cure myself in a different way. I said, "Once I start walking, I can eat. Then I am sure I can do without artificial help."

And what do you think? They called me to the office of the chief doctor and another doctor, and they asked why I had refused the treatment.

I told them that I was afraid and that I thought I could cure myself. He said, "What do you mean?"

I said, "Give me a chance for six months, and if after six months I still have water in my lungs, then I am going to do the treatment. I am going to do whatever you tell me to do; just give me the chance."

We were sleeping there with open windows during the winter. They covered us with many blankets. I can't stand heat. When it's very hot, I have to open the window. And he said, "OK. We'll give you medication, and we have to put you in bed with your head down and your legs up.

"Whatever you say, I am going to do." After six months, they took my x-ray and called me. The doctor said, "Congratulations." You believe that? "You really fixed yourself up. You have less water. Your tuberculosis is starting to shrink."

I said, "Thank you for giving me the opportunity." And I was still in the sanatorium. Then they sent us to another place. I don't remember the name. Anyway, we were free already. Like if I had money, I could go to Stockholm to visit, and they just kept us under supervision.

(*How did you get money?*) First of all, a rabbi came from America. They give us a little bit of money. We were looking terrific then. Our faces were red. He came during the Jewish holiday. He said, "You people don't have to fast on Yom Kippur. You are so sick, you have permission to eat."

Now, I don't think I ate anyway, just in memory of my parents. Funny thing, at home I ate on Yom Kippur, and after the war I wasn't eating. I am not eating, because this is the day for my parents and my sister. Then the rabbi said, "You know, you're like a rotten apple. It looks beautiful outside, but on the inside it's like you are."

And then he asked, "What do you think about the future?" If we wanted to go to Israel, he could arrange it. Many women went to Israel. When I was in Sweden, I started writing my memories, but my aunt in Bucharest destroyed it. Yes, I never forgave myself for letting her do that. I was writing; we didn't know what to do with ourselves anymore. Five times a day we ate, you believe it? Those breakfasts, you wouldn't believe. And we heard that some girl from Hungary, you wouldn't believe it, she opened the kitchen door with some keys to take the sweet biscuits out. They gave us so much to eat that stealing the food—this was really such a bad way to show them appreciation.

Oh, this started my things with Julian. I knew that his sister and my cousin were married, and I knew from her that Julian worked in the French government, in aviation. I knew from my cousin from before the war that Julian was working there, because she wanted very much for my sister to marry Julian. She was always talking about him. [Miriam didn't meet Julian until after the war.] As I mentioned before, her husband, my cousin, went to Russia. He was a Communist, and he was an engineer, building houses. They sent him to Siberia to build the bridges. Julian's sister went after him, and they had a baby. Her name was Klara, and the baby was Zosia. When the war started, they sent her back to Poland with the baby, and they killed my cousin because they said he was a Trotskyist. My cousin was studying in Prague in Czechoslovakia. Klara was—I think she was a chemist. She finished in college in Prague. And I knew all that, and I was hoping… I didn't know anything about my family. I was hoping I could find out from Julian what he knew about Klara, his sister. I wrote in French because I knew French from school. And they gave the letter to Julian. He started writing me letters. Then I found out he had also been in Auschwitz. He went to Russia from Auschwitz and went to Marseilles after that. And he wrote to me to come to France.

We started to live.

Before that, when I first came to Sweden, I sent a letter to my uncle in Bucharest, who was a very, very rich guy. He had three factories, and after I wrote to him, he said that everybody came from Poland to them but not my family. When Julian, wrote to me. I said, "Now is not the time to come to Paris." He said, "I understand you." Then after six months, my letter went to Russia, to Romania, to Bucharest. I received $500 from my uncle. He wrote to me, "Don't worry, we are going to make a visa saying you were born in Romania. We are going to bring you here. You know," he wrote, "You are our daughter." I remember I went to one Hungarian girl who was making money by sewing. I still have today the robe she made, such a dark red robe and blue. I don't have the blouse. She found a blouse with buttons. I wanted to go to Bucharest, you know, not looking like somebody from the camp.

They gave us things in Sweden. We were looking like idiots. There were two kinds of coats, three kinds of dresses. And then I started to see Sweden because I was rich. I had $500 dollars my uncle sent. We were seeing things in Sweden because my uncle arranged it. Stockholm, I love it, it's beautiful.

A few of my girls, I wrote to my uncle if I could invite them to my room, and he gave me permission. I invited them to go places with me. And then my visa was ready. I had to go to Czechoslovakia. I met two Jewish Romanian girls. I also wrote to my uncle that they were poor and asked him, "Why not take them with me to Czechoslovakia?" He wrote to me that it was OK. And we went to Czechoslovakia. We were living there maybe two weeks, waiting for permission to go to Hungary and to Romania.

And we had a wonderful time in Czechoslovakia. I remember the dark beer, and we were going to restaurants. This was something. We started to live. In Sweden we went to restaurants. I was always eating frankfurters with potatoes and milk. Such a funny thing: I love those gardens in Sweden. I tell you, I never was in such a garden in my life. I was just waiting for this paper to go to Czechoslovakia. And there were problems. They didn't want to let us go the way my uncle planned, that I take a plane in Prague and go to Bucharest. We couldn't do that. They said I had to go through Bulgaria. We had to take a train, and when we were in the train, these two girls and me, we met Romanian soldiers who were going back home. And they were helping us a lot because the train was stopping in different stations, and we had to go out and then take another train, and we had to go in and out, and then we had to go Bulgaria, until we came to the frontier, to Romania. This took a lot, even though I had papers and everything. One of the young soldiers, when we came to Romania, he called me. And my aunt said, "No more! You are not going to see those soldiers."

But what was the most important thing was the book that I wrote in Sweden. This was, you know—I brought this notebook. It was very heavy. When I came, my aunt first said, "This I am going to destroy. You have to forget everything." In her brain I could forget everything when she destroyed the book. And she destroyed my book.

(*Did you argue with her?*) I really don't remember. After, I couldn't forgive her or myself that I let her do that. Because even my cousin, her daughter, said to me, "You should fight with her." I don't remember how that was. You see, she was my aunt…She wasn't such a good… I shouldn't talk about the dead like that, *mashugana*. She was a very cold person, even to her daughter. I remember when I came to Bucharest, they were very rich. What can I tell you? My uncle was bringing her packages from the bank which still had paper around the money. She didn't know how much. She put this money in different places, and as she was such a person, the servant came and asked her to pay her more. She said, "No I cannot pay you more."

The woman went to my uncle and said, "I have to get paid more for my work." He said, "OK, I'll give you double, but don't tell Mrs. Gross (their name was Gross), because she would kill me."

When poor people came to the door, she was screaming murder: "Go to work." She never gave poor people money. But when she was in trouble, they ran from Romania to France; then she never let poor people in the Metro pass her without giving something. You see how you learn? When she had too much, she didn't give it; when she already had problems, she started to give money. She was lucky: her whole family before the war sent money to Switzerland because we knew that it was safe to have an account in Switzerland. And my uncle sent a lot of money to Switzerland because he knew what was going on in Bucharest and in Russia. You see, the guy who took my uncle's factory during the war, he gave this guy, the person who took care of his factory who was working for my uncle in normal times, he gave him this whole factory under his name. The Germans didn't touch him, and they gave my uncle and his family money to survive. After the Russians came, he had his factory back. But then the Russians took back the whole factory. He was lucky he had the money in Switzerland. He ran away to Paris, and he was living with this money.

7 Julian, George, Paris, New York

Before the Russians came, before my uncle went to Paris, I had a terrific year in Bucharest. I was constantly writing to Julian, and he always said, "Come to Paris. Come to Paris."

In the end, the Russians found out that I was born in Poland, and they sent the police and said I had to go back to Poland. Then my uncle had a false visa to Portugal made, and to go to Portugal, I had to go to Austria, to Vienna, and through France to Paris. But the train going to Poland was supposed to split in Budapest; half went to Vienna, and half went to Poland, I don't know where. And my uncle made arrangements; you know, money can do a lot. Then when the train stopped in Hungary, the guy who was conductor of the train took my luggage to the train to Austria and put me in this train. My uncle gave him a lot of money.

Now what happened was that they took me off the train, the Russian police, because we were in Hungary, which was also Russian, and they made me stay in the waiting room. I don't know why. They were looking at my papers. I said to this guy, to this conductor, to contact my uncle and let him know what was going on. I don't know what my uncle did, but in the end they put me back on the train, and the conductor took me to the train going to Austria. And I went to Austria and then to Paris. But I lost the sleeping room after they changed all that. In Paris, Julian was waiting for me at the station. And then I couldn't decide if I wanted to stay with Julian. It took time till I decided he was a really nice guy, and I needed somebody. I was looking for a father figure.

But anyway, I married Julian, and George was born. And I was very happy. I was always asking to have a son. I don't know why. I wanted him to be like my father. George wasn't like my father, but this was my dream. My father was six feet tall; George wasn't. My father was a sportsman; my son was a scholar—completely different. He did look a little bit like my father; something he had like my father—the jaws, the smile, his way of seeing life. You live today and money really means nothing, just to live better. Money is to be spent. My father was like that too.

We were in France maybe around five years, and Julian received the paper from his old uncle in New York to go to America. Then Julian said to me, "OK, you know what, I'll go for one year," because he could have permission from the government to take a one-year vacation leave. "And I'll see how it is. And if is OK, I'll send for you."

I said, "No way. Either we go together, or nobody goes." He said, "Then OK, I am going to go to the American consulate and tell them we don't want to go to America."

Everybody said, "You're crazy. After losing everybody, living in Europe is dangerous." When Julian said he didn't want to go, his uncle thought he was crazy for sure. He sent the visa again after maybe six months, and Julian was talking with his best friend, the doctor who took care of George when he was born. His friend said, "You're really crazy; you should go to the United States." We talked about it, and Julian said, "OK, then we'll all go together."

But you know, his uncle was a very old man. He wrote to Julian, "With your kind of job, in government, in aviation, with your diploma from the Sorbonne (Julian had three diplomas), I'm sure you can find a job." He sent the newspapers; they were looking for aviation, for engineering specialists. Julian knew seven languages. He didn't find one thing. You had to be a citizen to work in this kind of job. We came to America and Julian couldn't work, and this was the biggest tragedy. I was crying for one year. I was so sorry we came. I was sorry I didn't do what Julian said, to stay in Paris, to let him go alone. We couldn't go back. This was the worst thing. We had sold our apartment in Paris, and Julian had signed a letter—because he was working for the government, in aviation—that he wouldn't return to his job. This was a big regret, that he had no way to return. This was the real problem—that we couldn't go back, because he had to sign this letter and there was no job for him.

He went to work for something, I don't know, in a factory, really nothing. I was so afraid this was putting him down. He was saying nothing. We were living in his cousin's apartment in the Bronx, and it was really bad. Then we found a small apartment, and we moved to Washington Heights. George was getting bigger, and then George was very, very sick. When it comes to my mind, I think, maybe he had smallpox with complications. And he was very, very sick for many years. I remember this physician, a children's specialist. He came to our house many times in the evenings to give George an injection and medicine. He said, "Maybe I should put him in the hospital."

I said, "You think so?" He said, "I think the care that you give him he cannot have in the hospital. So maybe he better stay home." George survived, and then everything was OK. He just had problems with his eyes, and then much later, the doctor here in St. Joe's Hospital told us that his tumor had developed from childhood. Nobody knew that then. You didn't have the special machine that can check the brain, and he had times he couldn't see well. They prescribed glasses. And then he didn't need glasses. Later, before he died, he had problems with his eyes. I had to fight with him to go to the doctor, to the eye specialist. And the eye specialist sent him to another specialist, and they discovered the tumor. When the guy came from North Carolina (George got a graduate degree from the University of North Carolina) to talk about this memory gift for George, I said to him, "I want to tell you something. I have some kind of superstition." I was feeling then that the computer was doing something bad to George. George had three computers on his desk. He was working in research eighteen and a half years. I said, "George, this lighting from the computer is no good." He said, "Don't worry. You worry too much."

I was talking with the guy who works in research, and he said, "Mrs. Garvil, you're right. We know that doing research with the lights that come from the computer has to be changed. There is something there that we think is not good for the human body." He said, "You're right the way you think, because we feel the same way. We came to that conclusion. I'll send you the report, because we feel the same way." You see, George started the computer when he was fourteen years old. And we were so proud. He went every Saturday to learn, and this was a bad thing. I was talking Sunday with my girlfriend who was in the camp with me, who I haven't talked to in a whole year and a half. She lives in New York. I found her and her husband in New York when I got there. They came to the USA before us, and we were very good friends until I left New York. Even after we moved to Ann Arbor, we went back to New York because we missed our friends. And when George died, I felt she should be at his funeral. This was her place because I told her, if this would be your son, let's hope it never happens, I would say, "George, I have to be at Sophie's son's funeral." I felt very bad when she didn't come. I didn't want to talk to her. She called, and I said we had nothing to say to each other. I said I was feeling she was the one who should be here. She said circumstances were that she couldn't come. She sent me a card and said, "When you come to your peace, maybe you will remember me again."

This year I said to Julian, I'm going to send Sophie a card. He wasn't happy about it, because he said she had done things she wasn't supposed to do. Anyway, I sent her a card. She called me. She said, "I am not sending you a card; I just call people." We were talking maybe one hour. She said she was very happy that I called her. She understands me very well. She said, "Believe me, I couldn't come." I have to believe her. To me it wasn't a reason; to her it was a reason: this was in the middle of the divorce of her older son from his wife. She felt for him very much. I still feel she could have come for two days. Anyway, they are divorced now.

I can't sew very well. I went to drawing school in New York. I went for six months, and my work was on display. I have it still, my portfolio. I was doing that … You see, in my life, everything stopped. When I was doing well in school,

I found out I liked very much to do windows, to make arrangements by myself, colors, things like that. I loved it. I found a job at Barton's Candy in New York.

Our manager gave me some sketches so I could make this display with presents, with materials, with flowers. I loved it. And one day he said, "Go to the Fifth Avenue store, and make one window (there were six windows) by yourself." I didn't believe it. But you see, I was thinking, "I am on my way to a good career." I went to find dresses to stock the shop. And then I found out I had cataracts at a very young age. I was forty-two. This stopped me from my dream and my work.

My cataracts had some connection to when I didn't have enough to eat. What they gave us stopped our menstruation, at the concentration camp. And altogether that is why this came. The cataracts were bothering me so much. I didn't have the energy to continue working; you wouldn't believe it.

When I started drawing, I got something in my head, and I stayed up nights to draw dresses. I still have the dresses that I drew during those nights. As a child, I started drawing in school. We had drawing classes. I was always very good. I loved shades, you know. I was always good at these things. I love it. I always connect France to fashion. When I came to New York and could do that, I was very happy. We came there when George was three years old. Until he was three, I was home with him. I had time when George was small. Somehow all of my life came back to me. When Julian was working, they had a kindergarten and nurses and everything. Many times Julian would bring George with him. I started drawing plates, drawing children's stories like *Red Riding Hood* on plates and cups for kids. Then George started to be at home again. The guy was coming to my apartment to bring the plates and cups that I was drawing. This was always me, drawing, working with colors. I like fashion things even today.

I don't know if I told you— I had a call from my older cousin in Australia, and then I called the younger one two weeks later.

(*And you told him you are coming?*) I am not coming this year; next year, yes, I told him. He said, "Just look into health insurance because we don't accept American health insurance."

I was talking with people who said that when they buy tickets, they take some special insurance for Australia. This is what he's worried about. I like something to look forward to. This gives you a lift in life. Otherwise you feel tired. I am glad Julian wanted to go. He always loved to travel; he always wanted to go, go, go. He doesn't care about a house; he doesn't care about a car. When we came here, George said, "Maybe you buy a bigger house." He said "No, no, no, we will just be traveling." And we were traveling a lot in the beginning. We went every year for a few weeks to New York and back, and we went very often to Canada because Julian liked to talk French. We were traveling very much in the beginning when we came here. Gradually, we still were going twice a year someplace, summer or winter, but this wasn't so much like in the beginning. In the beginning it was during the year to Canada, during the year to New York. When we were in New York three weeks, it really wasn't in New York, because my friends don't live in New York. They live in other places like New Jersey and Long Island, and to be a little bit with each and to see each other, this takes time.

Funny thing, here's an important thing in my life. I don't know why it was so important, but it was. When I was a girl,

I wanted to be a librarian. And I had such a special place where I put all my books, like in a library. I put the cards inside when I loaned books to my friends. I put who the lender was. One of my preferred books was *Anne of Green Gables*. They show here [the United States] like two, three books in the series. I remember in Poland there were six books. My book was in Polish. When I was sick, I always went back to this book. I don't know why it had such a big influence on me. I'd be dreaming that I was like Anne. You'd be laughing, we were in New York, I was a grown-up woman with a child. I read in the paper that in the theater there would be *Anne of Green Gables*. I said to Julian, "You know what, everybody there will be just parents with kids, but you wouldn't mind to go just with me?" He said, "No! Let's go." I had a terrific time when I saw this show. Being already—not old, but a woman maybe I don't know, thirty-six, forty? It's the same feeling I have now when I tape all those stories from television. I really enjoy looking at them again. This book had a tremendous influence on me. When I talked with women, I heard that many women feel the same way about this book. I don't know why. Maybe the child that comes to this house and changes the lives of these two older people, maybe this has an effect. Maybe because she was such an outspoken person, and this really wasn't bad. Something amazing with this book. Very important in my life. I don't know why.

I used to read a lot. When I was young in Poland there was a time when I was reading things about people who came from other places and had to start life again. These were mostly books from Sweden, places like that. Then I had times when I was reading just Russian literature. I liked it very much. In fact I went to the same theater to see *Three Sisters*, Chekhov, I think. I don't know why I was reading so much. OK, there wasn't television. We had a very good radio, but you know, radio is radio. I remember Sunday we had two papers. One big paper was from the city, something like the Sunday *New York Times*. Sunday, when the paper came, we all got up, my father, my sister, and me. Sunday is still this way in my house. Julian loves to read. When the paper comes, we sit Sunday morning and read the paper.

When we came to New York, I met a woman who was George's girlfriend from school's mother. We were waiting for the kids to come from school, and I started to talk to her. And she was from Poland, from—oh I forgot the city. Anyway, we were talking. I told her I would love to go to the Metropolitan Museum of Art. It had art courses, and at that time I was working part time. I said I'd love to take those courses. She said, "I'll go with you. I was never inclined so much to art, but I would love to go." And we went for these courses. The teacher sent us to museums. And I'll never forget, we came to the museum, and I started telling her, "ah, Toulouse- Lautrec!" You know, believe me, I wasn't thinking about this thing during the war. After the war I was married with a child, going from one country to another, and this time was the time when I started to enjoy art again. It started to come to my head, Impressionism and Gauguin. I love it always. I started telling her, and she said, "How do you remember that?" And I said, "I have no idea—like something in my head, like drawers coming out." I was amazed myself. First of all, the colors caught me. This was always…not just colors, also the shape. Like Toulouse-Lautrec was like my drawings, color and girls dancing. Gauguin was colors, women mostly, with different colors, Asiatic women. And many, many things that I really like…ballet with Degas. You see, this is also movement, and dresses. This thing stayed in me from school. She said, "How do you remember all that?"

I said, "This is not my brain; this is my eyes. I think this is my eyes because I was active so much in fashion." When I see fashion on television, Julian sometimes says, "Oh, now it's fashion." I'll say, "Wait, wait, I have to see." I don't know; I'm always attracted to color, to movement, things like that. I think I'll be like that until I die.

I wanted to be a fashion designer. Sure, I sometimes have ideas during the night about dresses. You believe me; I sometimes couldn't sleep. I had to get up from bed and draw the dress. Then I slept. This is like me, when I want to say something to somebody, and I feel it is not right to say it the way I wanted, or maybe I am thinking wrong, I write. This gives me a terrific feeling. I can relax then. I have many things in my drawers that I never sent to people. I was writing what I was feeling about. It's the same way with my drawings, you know. I feel something, now it's just—I tell you, in my life it's been a thing that I wanted very dearly to do something, and sometimes a force stopped me. Like with my eyes, my whole career. I went to drawing school in New York. After six months in school, the teacher already put my drawings on display. I felt terrific. Suddenly came the cataracts, forty-something. Can you imagine? It took me so much to go to night school, to draw; I was really happy. I had gone to fashion school in Paris for three years. For me it was important to have something to do, like my mother did.

(*Didn't they operate on the cataracts?*) Yes, my, you see, this was terrible. One of my cataracts was operated on. They put me in a room with someone who was operated on for breast cancer, and she started to vomit. I have a nature that when I hear vomit, I vomit right away. This was all when I was forty-something. They didn't know that when they took the cataract part out, they should put in something else. They cut—the old system was that they cut the piece, and then they sewed. All the sewing, all the stitches burst in the night when I was vomiting. A doctor came; they called the doctor during the night. He said, "What are you doing?" I said, "I cannot hear vomit. When I hear vomit, I vomit." He was very, very mad about this. He was right; it was because of this that I now have glaucoma. You see, it was so bad you wouldn't believe it.

(*You got glaucoma then?*) No. Later, because of that. I remember when I came to the doctor, and I had something on my eye. He didn't tell me it was glaucoma. I saw after that what he wrote on the paper. After this accident he came to my house twice. This is not a doctor who goes to houses. He was usually just operating. And he came twice; he was afraid of what would happen to my eye. The right eye was very bad, and they didn't want to touch the left eye because of what had happened with the right one.

I went to maybe eight doctors, and no one wanted to take responsibility. These were the best doctors in New York City that we knew about. And then some friends called and told me that a doctor came from Spain, Dr. Castroviejo. He was the best. He was operating on the Pope in Rome. I went to him, he gave me his hand, and he said, "I promise nothing. I'll try to do my best." I said to him, I was crying, I said, "You are the first one who wants to do something." The whole operation he did without me sleeping, nothing. I didn't feel it because he put me on something. But he was telling me what he was doing. He was operating and he said, "One thing you have to promise me." He had his own small hospital on Fifth Avenue, where his patients were always staying. He said, "First of all, you have to stay one week in my hospital, then when you go home you have to promise me that you are going to do nothing, because this is the second operation on the same eye, and there is no tissue." He compared it to a sleeve. When you cut the sleeve, you cannot cover the arm anymore. An eye is the same way. When you look at my eye, you can see that it is partway out from the eye. He says, "Please, you have to be in bed or just sitting doing nothing."

I had a very good girlfriend in New York, Sophie, and she came to help me. In fact, her husband came to eat in our house because she wasn't home when she helped me in my house. I was lucky. Afterward, everything was OK. I was 20/20. I had vision in the left eye. I didn't know what to tell the doctor, how to thank him. I said, "You don't know what you have done for me."

The doctor is dead. His hospital building, his boat by some ocean, they're no more. When you went to his office, you saw students from Spain who he brought especially to see his patients. I met a girl who went to see him, and he put a whole artificial eye in her—oh, not artificial, somebody else's eye. Before I left the hospital, she could see. She was a young girl, such a nice-looking girl. She was so happy. When I was in his hospital, I couldn't sleep nights. One night I heard talking. Somebody rang the bell, and one of the nurses wanted to go open the door. Somebody said to her, "Don't you go; the old man doesn't like it. This is the eye that they bring from dead people. The old man has to do it himself to put it in its place, then he'll be sure it's OK. He doesn't let anybody do it."

I heard that ring, and what they were talking about was the doctor. You cannot find such a doctor today. And everybody knew him. When I came here, I went first to Dr. Smith for my cataracts. He knew about Castroviejo. Then I went to Dr. Winkleman, who also knew about Castroviejo. He was very, very well-known. He had his own hospital in Spain, in Madrid, and his hospital in New York.

But he didn't have a happy life. His wife left him because for him, work was everything. He was always occupied with his patients; this was his life. He was a terrific doctor, very rich, very unhappy. You know life sometimes. You can't have everything. You cannot. But now I worry because my eyes are getting worse. I don't see so well. It worries me, I think, that he's not alive anymore.

After George died, I was writing every day in a notebook, everything. A little bit about what I felt and a lot about what I had to do. Because when the lawyer came, he asked if I wanted to be executor with Julian. I said yes. First of all, I didn't realize what was meant by "executor." When I realized, I didn't know if I wanted to be. But the way I was thinking, it would be terrific for me to be occupied, because otherwise I'd be sitting there crying. I was twelve to thirteen hours on the phone, just to take care of this business of being executor. I am telling you, if you had told me in advance what I was supposed to do, I would have said, "Forget it, no way." But somewhere in life, when you have to do it, you do it. OK, I was looking a little for help from George's friends at General Motors. They would call and ask different things that weren't so easy for me. Because when I was starting to talk, I was starting to cry. People didn't know what I was talking about and what I was asking. His friends helped me a lot. The young guy that I told you about, he always called offices and things to find out what I was supposed to do. And it wasn't just to be executor, it was other things, like how to clean George's house, to take everything out, to sell his cars. There were so many things, not just being executor. Then, I tell you, I just couldn't live without Valium. I really couldn't.

When my cousins called me from Australia, this was such a big event for me. They both are not actually my cousins.

Their mother was my mother's first cousin. They were often in our house. We treated them like cousins. We were really close with them. I told you why the older one came very often, because this woman, our governess, was also in our family. He liked her very much; he came to visit her. He has one glass eye, which he has had for a long time. I didn't know when I was a girl that this eye was glass. When I was talking with the youngest cousin, he said to me that he was afraid he now had a cataract on the other good eye. I said, "A cataract today is nothing." He said, "Yes, but when you have one glass eye, you really worry." He isn't young anymore. He told me he's worried. I think after Thanksgiving I'll call there. I don't care what Julian says. He wants to go there, yes? How much money is he going to spend going to Australia? I told him, "You think it over." He said, "I don't know your cousin." I said, "Never mind, he's my second cousin."

You know what? Julian, he spoils me, because if I would tell him today I am going to buy a mink coat for twenty thousand dollars, he would say, "Go ahead." When I want something for me that's not important, he says, "Go ahead, buy it." But if I want to spend it this way, to go to Australia, he always says no. I don't know why. [Miriam did go to Australia to see her cousins in 1998, after Julian died.]

8 After Julian's Death

I had a full life, but it's sad that I am now alone. I think I learned a lot. In my life I had to learn a lot. My father spoiled me. I had to learn to live without my father. I was alone going to the concentration camp. When I talked to Sophie, we were talking about how we don't believe that was us in Auschwitz. Because when you think about it, you don't think it's possible. But it happened. I would never believe Sophie would die before me [Sophie died several years ago], because she had a stronger character. I even said to her son, "When I die before Sophie, you have to come to the cemetery." The worse thing is being old and alone.

Sometimes I felt very happy and sometimes very sad depending on what happened during my life. I had very happy times in my life and very sad times. I wish everyone would enjoy knowing how to take pleasure in good times. You should think that this is a nice life, and you should enjoy it. This is something that's a big gift, having this kind of pleasure in your life.

TIMELINE

May 23, 1921	Miriam Zack is born.
1938	Zack family leaves Lodz, moves to Dzialoszyce City.
Summer 1939	Miriam, her mother, and her sister are on the train to the camp. Her sister and mother are killed in Rava-Ruska. Her father dies at Auschwitz.
1942	Miriam enters Krakow-Plaszöw concentration camp.
1943	Miriam goes to Auschwitz.
1944	Miriam marches from Auschwitz to Bergen Belsen.
April 15, 1945	The English Army liberates Bergen Belsen. Miriam goes to Sweden.
1945	Miriam spends a year in Sweden.
1946	Miriam spends a year in Bucharest.
1947	Miriam goes to Paris.
1948	Miriam marries Julian Garvil.
1950	George Garvil is born.
1952	The Garvils move to New York City.
1977	Miriam and Julian move to Ann Arbor, Michigan.
1992	George Garvil dies.
May 12, 1995	Julian Garvil dies.

Miriam, her mother and sister, Lonya.

Miriam's mother, father and Lonya.

Miriam's mother, cousin Klara, her husband, and their baby Zosia.

SWEDEN AFTER THE WAR

Above and below: Miriam's friends, survivors from the camps.

Right: Miriam and her Swedish friend, Klara.

Sanitorium in Gothenburg, Sweden

Miriam in the new coat Klara and her friends gave her.
This is the picture she sent to Julian in Paris.

GEORGE GROWING UP

MIRIAM AND JULIAN

Made in the USA
Lexington, KY
11 April 2013